# NOW I GET IT!

## DIFFERENTIATE, ENGAGE, AND READ FOR DEEPER MEANING

*Judy Tilton Brunner*

Rowman & Littlefield Education
A division of
**ROWMAN & LITTLEFIELD PUBLISHERS, INC.**
*Lanham • New York • Toronto • Plymouth, UK*

Published by Rowman & Littlefield Education
A division of Rowman & Littlefield Publishers, Inc.
A wholly owned subsidiary of The Rowman & Littlefield Publishing Group, Inc.
4501 Forbes Boulevard, Suite 200, Lanham, Maryland 20706
www.rowman.com

Estover Road, Plymouth PL6 7PY, United Kingdom

British Library Cataloguing in Publication Information Available

**Library of Congress Cataloging-in-Publication Data**

Brunner, Judy Tilton
  Now I get it! : differentiate, engage, and read for deeper meaning /
Judy M. Brunner.
      pages cm
    Includes bibliographical references.
    ISBN 978-1-61048-612-5 (cloth : alk. paper) — ISBN 978-1-61048-613-2
    (pbk. : alk. paper) — ISBN 978-1-61048-614-9 (electronic)
    1. Reading comprehension—Study and teaching. I. Title.
  LB1050.45.B78 2012
  372.47—dc23                                                   2011052011

∞™ The paper used in this publication meets the minimum requirements
of American National Standard for Information Sciences—Permanence of
Paper for Printed Library Materials, ANSI/NISO Z39.48-1992.

Printed in the United States of America

For Alex, Brady, and Baby Brunner—
three very wonderful additions to our family.

# CONTENTS

CONTENTS

# PREFACE

Every day I am inspired. I am inspired by teachers of the past. I am inspired by teachers of the present. I am also inspired by future educators enrolled in my classes at Missouri State University that hope someday to be teachers, principals, counselors, and superintendents. They want to be part of the community of professional educators.

As I reflect on thirty-plus years as a teacher and principal, I am reminded of all those that have gone before to help pave the way for an educational environment worthy of our twenty-first century students. The kids today really are different, and they deserve nothing less than our very best.

Getting students excited about reading is possible, and it involves working smarter, not harder. Teachers need to provide strategic, direct instruction about why the material is important, and in every way possible, prepare students to succeed. They also need strategies that differentiate, engage, and require students to read for deeper meaning. Professional development in literacy and use of the latest research and strategies both help to ensure student success (Brunner, 2009).

While I do not necessarily believe every teacher is a teacher of reading, what I do believe is all teachers—regardless of content and/ or grade level—need to know how to support learning while students read difficult and challenging text. Hopefully, the strategies contained within this book will provide an appropriate framework for understanding and specific ways to facilitate instruction.

I was recently asked to respond to the statement, "Today's students are not the students we were trained to teach." My response was simple and straightforward. "That's right. They are much smarter!" We must be smarter, too.

Prepare well, and enjoy each day!

# FOREWORD

It is hard to disagree that being an educator is extremely challenging these days. In fact, education is in a state of flux due to the number of entities, from political leaders to CEOs of major corporations, all believing they have a say in the way education ought to occur in schools. While there are varying opinions about what is the best way to *improve* education, we must all continue to focus on doing what is best for each individual learner. The potential for an evolution of our educational system is greater than at any time in history. It is, indeed, an exciting time to be an educator.

Today's student is wired differently due to the amount of exposure to digital text, including thousands of text messages, Facebook posts, tweets, images from video games, commercials, YouTube videos, and music. Students expect quick responses to questions and instant gratification. As a result, student ability to read, understand, and apply content is a matter of survival in a competitive world.

With the increase in the amount of information at students' disposal, it is even more important for schools to teach students how to read for understanding. But, when does this happen? What strategies are to be used to teach students to become independent readers? Should every teacher be a trained literacy teacher? What about teaching the content? These are questions many principals, literacy coaches, teachers, and curriculum coordinators are asking, and asking often.

In *Now I Get It! Differentiate, Engage, and Read for Deeper Meaning*, Judy Brunner answers these questions and more while demonstrating an understanding of the time constraints, pressure, and accountability that educators face: from the elementary level to post-secondary and graduate instructors. As a principal of a large suburban high school of nearly 2,400 students, I am keenly aware of the wide array of reading levels of students. Some are reading well above the twelfth grade while others struggle at an elementary reading level. On some occasions, these students are in the same classroom.

Many teachers know and understand *what* they need to do and *why* they need to do it, which is to improve their students' reading level, but the question that this book answers is *how* to do it. This book not only answers the *how to* question for teachers, but also for principals, literacy coaches, and curriculum coordinators. Reading is not only fundamental; it is foundational to today's students as they face many unknowns in terms of career and college readiness. As educators, it is our duty and moral obligation to give students the tools to navigate through traditional and digital texts they are exposed to daily. The ability to read, and read well, is the one tool all students need.

Be Great,
Dwight Carter, Principal
Gahanna Lincoln High School

# ABOUT THIS BOOK

Over the course of my educational career I was fortunate to participate in a number of excellent staff development opportunities. It was evident many subjects deserved investigation and inclusion in the vast array of topics related to continuing education. As educators at all levels recognize, knowledge of literacy strategies continues to be an area of critical need for teachers and administrators. For that reason, I decided to expand the resources provided in *I Don't Get It! Helping Students Understand What They Read*. While a few of my favorite techniques are included in both, most strategies in this book are different. Additionally, suggestions for differentiating instruction and expanded ideas for the use of technology are provided to the reader.

As a former special education teacher, as well as an elementary, middle, and high school principal, one of my biggest concerns was the number of students that appeared to be disengaged from the academic environment primarily because, for them, reading a textbook was an overwhelming, if not impossible, task. I also saw many well-meaning teachers struggle with how to help those students understand, remember, and use information acquired from nonfiction expository texts. Teachers were frustrated, kids were mentally "dropping out," and principals and parents were discouraged.

Whether helping a teacher during a formative evaluation, teaching university students specific methodologies, or providing on-site training for professional educators, my "audience" has always seemed to want two things:

1. Strategies that were simple to implement
2. Strategies that work in a real classroom with real students

With this in mind, the book is straightforward, simply written, and direct with its intent and content.

## THE GOALS OF THIS BOOK

In writing this instructional resource, it was my hope to accomplish four things. First, the book is in a format that is user-friendly. Busy professionals need to have something easily referenced when faced with challenging and difficult dilemmas related to reading and literacy.

Second, it is important the recommended strategies not be too difficult to implement. Readers of this book will likely be from a variety of educational backgrounds; they will want techniques they can understand and, most importantly, utilize *now*. It should not be necessary for the reader to have an advanced degree in reading in order to understand and apply the contents of each section.

Third, the book should be both practical and affordable for individuals with limited time and financial resources. Educators want strategies that are manageable in terms of time and money.

Finally, some strategies are applicable and helpful in the post-secondary classroom, whether that instruction is occurring in a community college setting or on the campus of a major university. The types of reading that college students are required to remember and understand are complex and rigorous. Consequently, notations have been made indicating teaching methods that are also appropriate in a post-secondary setting.

To that end, I believe this book has accomplished the aforementioned goals. The selected strategies placed within this text have been carefully considered for their ease of use, utility in terms of differentiation, and simplicity of format. The book can be read cover to cover, "on the run," or as a resource in response to a specific, expressed need by teaching staff. Regardless of the reason for reading the content, the book will provide practical, effective, and research-based strategies to help students read, understand, and remember the text.

## WHO THIS BOOK IS FOR

The book is for teachers and literacy coaches of all students, in all grades and subjects. The strategies will be useful as teaching tools for a classroom with a wide range of cognitive abilities. In fact, that may be the book's greatest strength. With educator accountability at an all time high, the use of the suggested strategies will provide a framework for meaningful instruction related to reading comprehension and vocabulary development for *all* students. The suggested strategies should produce positive results related to academic achievement and student engagement.

This book is also written for principals needing a resource for teachers struggling with how to support reading comprehension. Since reading is at the base of most academic endeavors, it is critically important for principals to have sources at their disposal that help teachers differentiate and prepare for instruction in the twenty-first century. If school administrators are to be instructional leaders, they need the appropriate tools to accomplish the task.

This book is also for graduate and undergraduate university students pursuing teaching credentials. Regardless of the content area, the book has merit for any pre-service or practicing educator that uses print as an instructional tool. Additionally, it can be used by post-secondary educators as they facilitate learning for their own students.

This book is also for parents. As a child's "first teacher," parents want specific ways to help children navigate the challenge of a difficult textbook. Whether it is an electronic resource from the Internet or a district adopted text, after reading this book, parents will have a number of ways to help students "make the grade" in terms of reading achievement.

## OVERVIEW OF THE CONTENTS

The book is divided into three sections. Section 1 includes a variety of strategies related to vocabulary. While most reading experts agree vocabulary development is important to understanding the written word, many educators lack knowledge of specific ways they can help students expand their personal lexicons related to topics and subject areas. Teachers need to do more than merely use the glossary of a text to define a term. Teaching vocabulary is a critical component of activating a reader's background knowledge; thus, a number of vocabulary strategies are included. With few exceptions, these strategies will engage readers of all ages.

Section 2 includes a number of techniques designed to help with reading comprehension. These strategies will support students as they read fiction, non-fiction, and expository passages.

Section 3 includes strategies to help support students as they develop and mature into independent readers and learners. While the teaching strategies in this chapter support both vocabulary development and reading comprehension, they specifically help students become life-long and self-motivated learners.

## THE FORMAT

The explanation of each strategy includes the following:

- Why Use the Strategy?
- Types of Texts
- Grade Level Adaptability

- Steps in the Process
- Engage with Bloom's Taxonomy
- Benefits
- Considerations
- Suggestions for Differentiation
- Technology Adaptation
- Teacher Notes

Many of the strategies included in this book are applicable at most levels of Bloom's Taxonomy (Anderson and Krathwohl, 2001). However, readers should remember the highest levels of thinking—applying, analyzing, and evaluating—occur only when the teacher consciously structures questions accordingly.

The technology adaptation for some strategies has been included for two primary reasons. First, technology is appealing to students and teachers. It sparks an interest when the learner might otherwise disengage. Second, the use of online resources adds a dimension to learning both vast and global. However, because many schools have limited technological assets, all strategies can be implemented without the use of an electronic resource.

## MODIFY AND ADAPT

While this book is written with a step-by-step process, educators must adapt and make adjustments to the strategies when it makes sense to do so. Teachers understand individual student needs and should use professional judgment when choosing methods for implementation, modifications of techniques, and grade level adaptability.

# VOCABULARY

Words matter. In particular, the *understanding* of *vocabulary words* matters, and educators have always known the highest achieving students will probably be the ones with the richest and most extensive vocabularies. In 1968, the National Council of Teachers of English proposed, "Because of the verbal nature of most classroom activities, knowledge of words and the ability to use language are essential to success in these activities. After schooling has ended, adequacy of vocabulary is almost equally essential for achievement in vocations and in society."

Regardless of the universally held belief that learning vocabulary is of critical importance, classroom teachers across the content areas continue to rely on instructional methods that are not necessarily effective or engaging. While there may be a variety of reasons for this disconnect, educators need a systematic approach to the vocabulary development of all students.

Educators must remember they are teaching students in the twenty-first century. These young people want fast-paced answers and variety of experience. While learners in the past may have been satisfied with a fifty-mile-per-hour pace, students today expect to go from zero to one hundred in ten seconds or less. Though some instructional objectives do not necessarily lend themselves to instant gratification, to ignore learning styles and preferences would be less than productive and self-defeating in today's classroom. The suggested strategies in this chapter provide variety, differentiation, and academic engagement. In other words, students like them.

Each curricular area has commonly associated words as well as other less frequently used terms no less important to student understanding of content. There will always be words that need to be taught by teachers and learned by students. The following strategies are student-friendly and well grounded in educational research and should be used as a framework for instruction.

## STRATEGY: ADMIT AND EXIT SLIPS

### Why Use the Admit and Exit Slips Strategy?

The primary purpose of the Admit and Exit Slips Strategy (Vacca and Vacca, 2008) is to help students organize their thoughts prior to coming to class or as they are preparing to leave. As vocabulary strategies, they can provide a way for students to learn a manageable amount of terms or vocabulary words in a limited amount of time.

### Types of Texts

Fiction, Non-Fiction, and Expository Text. This strategy can be easily modified for a variety of content areas.

### Grade Level Adaptability

Elementary and Secondary.

### Steps in the Process

1. Direct students to write vocabulary words and definitions in their own words using individual index cards for each word.
2. Ask students to draw a non-linguistic representation for all terms and words on the backside of the note card.

3. Repeat this activity daily during the instructional unit until all vocabulary words are included.
4. Instruct students to turn in words at end or beginning of designated class (admit slips at beginning of class and exit slips at the conclusion of class).
5. Encourage students to use vocabulary cards as a study guide.

## Engage with Bloom's Taxonomy

- *Remember:* Define each vocabulary word.
- *Understand:* Provide a description, explanation, or example of the term.
- *Apply:* Group the words, and label each group. Compare groupings with classmates.
- *Analyze:* What other related words could be part of this instructional unit? How are these words similar to the existing words? How are they different?
- *Evaluate:* Prioritize the words related to the topic. Which words are most important to the understanding of the concept(s)?

## Benefits

- Provides a novel idea replacing the idea of "homework"
- Provides a ready-made study guide
- Incremental learning
- Encourages acquisition of a mental image of word
- Applicable for a variety of subjects
- Easily implemented in a classroom for students with a wide range of academic ability

## Considerations

- None noted.

## Suggestions for Differentiation

- Provide different words to students.
- Allow students to share cards with other students.

- Collect cards at the end of the unit and place them in a learning center for reinforcement and review.
- Have students keep a vocabulary notebook of new terms. Students would individually decide which terms to include.
- Use the cards with a competitive game such as Concentration.

## Technology Adaptation

1. Students may use an electronic dictionary or thesaurus to verify the meaning of terms.
2. Students may use Glogster to create virtual posters of vocabulary words.
3. Students may use Twitter or Edmodo to share words and definitions with classmates.

## Teacher Notes

_____

_____

_____

_____

_____

_____

_____

_____

_____

## STRATEGY: CLUSTER CONNECTION

## Why Use Cluster Connection Strategy?

The Cluster Connection Strategy (Brunner, 2011) is designed to help students understand differences, similarities, and shades of meanings related to specific vocabulary words. It encourages students to consider the relationships between vocabulary words.

## Types of Texts

Fiction, Non-Fiction, and Expository Text. This strategy can be easily modified for a variety of content areas.

## Grade Level Adaptability

Elementary, Secondary, and Post-Secondary.

## Steps in the Process

1. Choose vocabulary words from the text.
2. Ask students to draw a small circle that includes the word and place the circle at the top of a sheet of paper.
3. Ask students to use a thesaurus, glossary, or dictionary to make a word web using synonyms of the vocabulary word. Ask students to design a Cluster Connection for each vocabulary word.
4. After webs are complete, ask students to collaborate with another student while sharing synonyms for each word. The discussion should include how synonyms may or may not slightly change the meaning of a word or term.

## Engage with Bloom's Taxonomy

- *Remember:* What is a ___? Can you recall ___?
- *Understand:* What is the best choice of words for ___? Using your own words, define ___.
- *Apply:* How do these words relate to the overall content of the chapter?
- *Analyze:* How are the words related to each other? Do they have similar prefixes, suffixes, or root words?
- *Evaluate:* What was your reasoning when you selected your words for the graphic organizer? Are some synonyms better than others? If so, why are they better?

## Benefits

- Can be done individually or with a small group
- Requires little advance preparation from the teacher

- Can be easily implemented by a substitute teacher
- Facilitates differentiation depending on words provided to students
- Familiarizes students with how to use a thesaurus, dictionary, or glossary

## Considerations

- This strategy may be too time consuming to do with all vocabulary words.

## Suggestions for Differentiation

- Provide different words or vary the number of vocabulary words.
- Allow some students to work individually while others work with peers.
- Ask students to provide a non-linguistic representation of selected vocabulary words.
- Have students keep a vocabulary notebook of new terms. Students would individually decide which terms to include.

## Technology Adaptation

1. Have students create the word webs electronically.
2. Encourage the use of an electronic dictionary or thesaurus.
3. Use classroom blogs to give feedback to students related to the choice of words within the graphic organizer, complexity of chosen words, and how each word supports the understanding of text content.

## Teacher Notes

_____

_____

_____

_____

_____

_____

_____

_____

## STRATEGY: CONCEPT CIRCLES

### Why Use the Concept Circles Strategy?

The primary purpose of the Concept Circles Strategy (Vacca and Vacca, 2008) is to help students understand the relationships between words and to support critical analysis of text.

### Types of Texts

Fiction, Non-Fiction, and Expository Text. This strategy can be easily modified for a variety of content areas.

### Grade Level Adaptability

Elementary, Secondary, and Post-Secondary.

### Steps in the Process

1. Direct students to divide a circle into four (or more) sections.
2. Provide words or phrases for the quadrants.
3. Use Concept Circles in a variety of ways.
   - All of the words in the circle are related and the students must tell how they are related.
   - All of the words in the circle are related except one. Students are asked to identify the word or phrase that does not "fit."
   - Leave quadrant(s) blank and direct students to fill in the blank sections with related words.

- Students should be prepared to explain why they chose words or phrases and how words are related or not related.

## Engage with Bloom's Taxonomy

- *Remember:* Define the words in each quadrant.
- *Understand:* Describe how the words are related. How are the words similar? How are the words different? If you were to label the words in the circle, what label(s) would you use?
- *Apply:* Use the words in the quadrants in a sentence. If these words were used in a paragraph, what might be the main idea of the text?
- *Analyze:* What other related words could be placed in each quadrant? How are these words similar to the existing words? How are they different?
- *Evaluate:* Prioritize the words related to the topic. Which words are most important to the understanding of the concept(s)?

## Benefits

- Encourages a deeper understanding of the term and/or concept
- Encourages active involvement rather than passive memorization of key terms
- Can be done individually, in small groups, or with the whole class
- Applicable for a variety of subjects
- Can be easily implemented in a classroom for students with a wide range of academic ability

## Considerations

- Some students may not understand some of the related words.
- Some students may need assistance in activating background knowledge related to the vocabulary word or term.
- The strategy may be too time-consuming to use for each concept or for all vocabulary words.

## Suggestions for Differentiation

- Provide different words or vary the number of Concept Circles provided to students.
- Allow students to work individually or in small groups.
- Provide students the option of expanding the number of sections within the Circle. (Each Circle should have a minimum of four sections.)
- Allow students to make their own Concept Circles based on lesson content. Students can share these Circles with classmates.
- Have students keep a vocabulary notebook of new terms. Students individually decide which terms to include.

## Technology Adaptation

1. Students may use an electronic dictionary or thesaurus to verify the meaning of terms.
2. Students may create colorful text boxes through the use of a computer to display the Concept Circles.
3. Students may use Twitter to critique Concept Circles created by classmates.

## Teacher Notes

_____

_____

_____

_____

_____

_____

_____

## STRATEGY: CONCEPT OF DEFINITION MAPPING

### Why Use the Concept of Definition Mapping Strategy?

The primary purpose of the Concept of Definition Mapping Strategy (Schwartz and Raphael, 1985) is to assist students in understanding the meaning of key vocabulary words. Through the use of a graphic organizer, this strategy will assist students with a deeper understanding of key terms.

### Types of Texts

Fiction, Non-Fiction, and Expository Text. This strategy can be easily modified for a variety of content areas.

### Grade Level Adaptability

Elementary, Secondary, and Post-Secondary.

### Steps in the Process

1. Identify key terms from the text.
2. For each word on the list, write the word on the board or have students write the word in the middle of a sheet of paper.
3. While skimming the chapter's content, ask students to look for the word and relevant information related to the word. Encourage students to use glossaries, indexes, text features, and table of contents to help locate important information.
4. The teacher and/or students should then create a word map of related terminology.

### Engage with Bloom's Taxonomy

- *Remember:* What is a _____? What do I know about _____?
- *Understand:* Provide a definition for _____? What are some synonyms for _____?
- *Apply:* What is an example of _____? How could you illustrate _____?

- *Analyze:* Compare and contrast the student created Concept of Definition Maps.
- *Evaluate:* Critique the student created maps with or without a scoring rubric.

## Benefits

- Encourages a deeper understanding of the term and/or concept
- Active involvement rather than passive memorization of key terms
- Utilizes text structure to support learning
- Can be done individually, in small groups, or with the whole class
- Applicable for a variety of subjects
- Relative ease of planning for teacher
- Prepares students for independent reading
- Easily implemented in a classroom for students with a wide range of academic ability

## Considerations

- Some students may not understand some of the related words.
- Some students may need assistance in activating background knowledge related to the vocabulary word or term.

## Suggestions for Differentiation

- Have students keep a vocabulary notebook of new terms. Students would individually decide which terms to include.
- Use differentiated scoring rubrics.
- Allow students to work individually or in small groups.
- Provide a partially completed definition map for some students.

## Technology Adaptation

1. Students may use an electronic dictionary or thesaurus to verify the meaning of terms.
2. Students may create colorful text boxes or use Glogster to display the Definition Map.

3.  Use an electronic word search puzzle to provide for introduction or review of words.

## Teacher Notes

_____

_____

_____

_____

_____

_____

_____

_____

## STRATEGY: CONTEXTUAL REDEFINITION

### Why Use the Contextual Redefinition Strategy?

The purpose of the Contextual Redefinition Strategy (Readance, Bean, and Baldwin, 1998) is to assist students with contextual analysis by helping them make educated guesses related to the meaning of a specific word. By using the steps in the process of this strategy students will be better prepared to read efficiently and proficiently without teacher assistance.

### Types of Texts

Fiction, Non-Fiction, and Expository Text. This strategy can be easily modified for a variety of content areas.

### Grade Level Adaptability

Elementary, Secondary, and Post-Secondary.

## Steps in the Process

1. Select unfamiliar vocabulary words from the reading.
2. Write a sentence that includes each word. The sentence should give clues to the meaning of the vocabulary word.
3. Divide students into small groups.
4. Present individual words to groups of students. This can be done with a whiteboard, transparency, PowerPoint, or on paper. In some cases, it may help to pronounce each word for the students.
5. Instruct students to define each word based on background knowledge and be prepared to explain why the definition is correct.
6. After students have finished providing their own definitions, give each group vocabulary words in the context of how they appear in the reading.
7. If necessary, ask students to use the sentence to modify previous definitions.
8. After modifications are made, direct students to verify definitions using the glossary or dictionary.

## Engage with Bloom's Taxonomy

- *Remember:* Define the vocabulary words. Recognize the vocabulary words in the context of the selected reading.
- *Understand:* Use the vocabulary words in a new sentence. Discuss how each vocabulary word fits within the context of the instructional objectives. List examples or synonyms for each vocabulary word.
- *Apply:* What are some examples of the words? How can the words be used to demonstrate understanding of the text content?
- *Analyze:* Make two or more groupings of the vocabulary words. What would be a label for each group? Ask students to prioritize words related to their overall importance in understanding the concept of the text. Justify the choice of the original definition.

- *Evaluate:* Justify the choice of the original definition. Critique the original definitions of classmates.

## Benefits

- Provides a structure for teaching students how to use context clues to decode and understand challenging text
- Provides teacher flexibility and opportunity to differentiate instruction depending on the words given to each group
- Facilitates a deeper understanding of the text
- Actively engages students in the process of deliberation
- Encourages student collaboration
- Prepares students for independent reading
- Provides a framework for a civil and respectful discussion

## Considerations

- If students are unfamiliar with many of the vocabulary words, the activity will have limited success.

## Suggestions for Differentiation

- Provide different words or vary the number of words and sentences provided to students.
- Allow students to work individually or in small groups.
- Provide students with twenty-five words and sentences with instructions that they are to choose twenty words and sentences in order to define and redefine.
- Have students keep a vocabulary notebook of new terms. Students individually decide which terms to include.

## Technology Adaptation

1. Have small groups of students work at a computer to brainstorm ideas or consult an online dictionary.
2. Display student ideas to generate whole class discussion by using a projector.

3. Assign different words to individual groups and ask students to share their definitions and redefinitions on a class blog.
4. After definitions have been finalized, ask students to create an electronic study guide of terms.

## Teacher Notes

_____

_____

_____

_____

_____

_____

_____

_____

## STRATEGY: EXCLUSION BRAINSTORMING

### Why Exclusion Brainstorming Strategy?

The purpose of the Exclusion Brainstorming Strategy (Blachowicz, 1986) is to assist students as they think about words and ideas they already know related to a specific topic. It will also provide students the opportunity to explore a controversial topic while differentiating points of view and formulating opinions based on relevant information. This strategy promotes engagement and encourages critical and complex thinking.

### Types of Texts

Fiction, Non-Fiction, and Expository Text. This strategy can be easily modified for a variety of content areas.

## Grade Level Adaptability

Elementary, Secondary, and Post-Secondary.

## Steps in the Process

1. Display the title of the reading selection for all students to see.
2. Under the title of the selection, list five words or phrases related to the topic, five words or phrases that are not related to the topic, and five ambiguous words or phrases. These words or phrases should be listed randomly.
3. Ask students to eliminate any words or phrases they believe are not related to the topic.
4. Ask students to select words or phrases they believe are most likely to appear in the reading selection.
5. Ask students to list words they believe may be ambiguous.
6. Explain that all students should be prepared to justify choices.
7. Assign the reading to the students and tell them the purpose for reading will be to see if previous selections were accurate.
8. After students have completed reading material, facilitate a discussion of the content. Ask them to generate their own selection of related, unrelated, or ambiguous terms.

## Engage with Bloom's Taxonomy

- *Remember:* Define and memorize the definitions of each vocabulary word.
- *Understand:* Restate or rephrase the definitions for each word.
- *Apply:* After eliminating the unrelated words, use the remaining words in sentences that demonstrate understanding of the definition and relationship to the text.
- *Analyze:* Explain the process used to eliminate specific words. What other words could be added to each category?
- *Evaluate:* After new words are added, critique the words selected by classmates. Which words are most important to understanding the overall content of the text?

## Benefits

- Easy to facilitate and implement
- Promotes student engagement
- Supports readers that may need additional teacher assistance
- Applicable for a variety of subjects
- Activates background knowledge
- Facilitates critical thinking
- Provides a specific purpose for reading the text
- Can be done individually, in small groups, or with whole class

## Considerations

- If students have little background knowledge on the topic, the discussion of terms and phrases may not be productive.
- Teacher preparation time is needed to choose appropriate words and phrases.

## Suggestions for Differentiation

- Choose words of varying complexity for student groups.
- Allow students to work individually or with a small group.
- Give students a choice of using online resources, text glossary, or interview with parents, classmates, or others to determine which words should be placed into which group. Discuss which resource provided the most accurate information.
- Display groups of words electronically with pictures and/or illustrations.
- Display groups of words on paper including a non-linguistic representation.
- Have students keep a vocabulary notebook of new terms. Students individually decide which terms to include.

## Technology Adaptation

1. Display the chosen words or phrases with a projector.
2. Ask students to email choices to the teacher so a master listing can be compiled and electronically displayed.

3. Ask students to use the Internet to electronically brainstorm the terms and phrases.
4. Use Glogster to display groups of words.

**Teacher Notes**

_____

_____

_____

_____

_____

_____

_____

_____

## STRATEGY: GRAPHIC ORGANIZERS

### Why Use the Graphic Organizers Strategy?

The primary purpose of the Graphic Organizers Strategy (Vacca and Vacca, 2008) is to help students understand the relationships between words and ideas.

### Types of Texts

Fiction, Non-Fiction, and Expository Text. This strategy can be easily modified for a variety of content areas.

### Grade Level Adaptability

Elementary, Secondary, and Post-Secondary.

### Steps in the Process

1. Review vocabulary words looking for the ones most helpful in understanding instructional objectives.

2. Arrange the words in a manner that shows interrelationships between words and concepts.
3. Add words that will help students understand the instructional objectives.
4. Ask students to work with a partner to discuss the terms and connection between words, as depicted in the graphic organizer.
5. Ask students to evaluate the organizer related to their understanding of the content. State that terms can be rearranged if it makes sense to do so.
6. Work in groups or as a whole class to expand the organizer. Organizers should be expanded as necessary throughout the instructional unit.

## Engage with Bloom's Taxonomy

- *Remember:* Define each vocabulary word.
- *Understand:* Provide a description, explanation, or example of the term. Explain the relationship between words.
- *Apply:* Regroup the words, and label each group. Compare groupings with classmates.
- *Analyze:* What other related words could be part of this instructional unit? How are these words similar to the existing words? How are they different? Provide only the vocabulary words, and ask students to create their own graphic organizers.
- *Evaluate:* Prioritize the words related to the topic. Which words are most important to the understanding of the concept(s)? Post student organizers around the room. Provide each student or a pair of students a scoring rubric, and ask them to evaluate how well the graphic organizer communicates an understanding of the concepts.

## Benefits

- Ready-made study guide
- Good pre-reading, during reading, or post-reading activity
- Applicable for a variety of subjects
- Easily implemented in a classroom for students with a wide range of academic ability

- Provides for active participation from all students
- Can be easily implemented by a substitute teacher
- Supports visual learners
- Explanation of graphic organizers by students supports auditory learners

## Considerations

- This strategy may be too time consuming for use with all vocabulary words.

## Suggestions for Differentiation

- Provide different words to some students.
- Allow students to share organizers with other students.
- Collect organizers at the end of the unit and place them in a learning center for reinforcement and review.
- Have students keep a vocabulary notebook of new terms. Students individually decide which terms to include.
- Ask students to use symbols, as well as words, in the graphic organizer.

## Technology Adaptation

1. Students may use an electronic dictionary or thesaurus to verify the meaning of terms.
2. Use Glogster to create virtual posters of organizers.
3. Students may use Twitter or Edmodo to share words and definitions with classmates.
4. Use an animated PowerPoint presentation to explain the graphic organizer.

## Teacher Notes

_____

_____

_____

_____

_____

_____

_____

_____

## STRATEGY: KNOWLEDGE RATING SCALE

### Why Use the Knowledge Rating Scale Strategy?

The purpose of the Knowledge Rating Scale Strategy (Blachowicz, 1986) is to provide a way to introduce unknown words to students. This strategy activates background knowledge and helps students connect new information to what they already know.

### Types of Texts

Fiction, Non-Fiction, and Expository Text. This strategy can be easily modified for a variety of content areas.

### Grade Level Adaptability

Elementary, Secondary, and Post-Secondary.

### Steps in the Process

1. Select important vocabulary words from the reading.
2. Prepare a handout for students including each vocabulary word or phrase followed by three columns labeled "Know It Well," "Have Heard or Seen It," and "No Clue."
3. Divide the class into groups of 2–4 students, and ask them to share what they know about the topic or words.
4. Ask students to review each word or phrase, and place a check mark in the appropriate column next to the word.
5. After students have completed the Knowledge Rating Scale for each word, ask them to write sentences for words listed in the "Know It Well" column.

6. Direct students to read the text. After completion of the reading, ask them to add definitions for unknown words as well as confirm or modify their previous listing.
7. If time allows, instruct students to write sentences using the remaining vocabulary words.

## Engage with Bloom's Taxonomy

- *Remember:* Define the words in the "Know It Well" category. Pronounce the words in all categories.
- *Understand:* Define the words you know well in your own words. After all words have been learned, choose some of the vocabulary words and write a paragraph that demonstrates understanding of each term.
- *Apply:* After studying the content, what additional words could be added in the "Know It Well" category?
- *Analyze:* After all vocabulary words have been defined, ask students to categorize the words and label the categories.
- *Evaluate:* After all vocabulary words have been defined, ask students to prioritize the words according to importance within the context of the instructional objectives. Students should be prepared to justify their choices.

## Benefits

- Activates background knowledge
- Applicable for a variety of subjects
- Provides teacher flexibility and the opportunity to differentiate instruction
- Provides a purpose for reading
- Connects new vocabulary to what students already know
- Can be easily implemented by a substitute teacher
- Requires limited teacher preparation
- Straightforward and easy to explain and understand
- Can be done individually or with small groups

## Considerations

- If students lack background knowledge, it may be difficult for them to engage and participate.

## Suggestions for Differentiation

- Choose words of varying complexity for student groups.
- Allow students to work individually or with a small group.
- Display groups of words electronically with pictures and/or illustrations.
- Display groups of words on paper including a non-linguistic representation.
- Suggest students make a non-linguistic representation for selected vocabulary words.
- Have students keep a vocabulary notebook of new terms. Students individually decide which terms to include.

## Technology Adaptation

1. Ask students to use an electronic table or spreadsheet to make the graphic organizer.
2. Have students design an electronic presentation that includes vocabulary words and sentences. Encourage creativity related to sentences, color, design, etc.

## Teacher Notes

_____

_____

_____

_____

_____

_____

_____

## STRATEGY: KNOWNS AND UNKNOWNS

### Why Use the Knowns and Unknowns Strategy?

The Knowns and Unknowns Strategy was designed to support students as they formulate inferences and construct word meanings based on text.

### Types of Texts

Fiction, Non-Fiction, and Expository Text. This strategy can be easily modified for a variety of content areas.

### Grade Level Adaptability

Elementary, Secondary, and Post-Secondary.

### Steps in the Process

1. Ask students to choose words that are unfamiliar.
2. Direct students to predict the word's meaning and make a list of each word and definition. This listing should include what types of "clues" were used to make the prediction.
3. Direct students to share their words, predicted definitions, and "clues" with classmates.
4. After discussion, ask students to verify the correct definitions using the glossary or an online dictionary.

### Engage with Bloom's Taxonomy

- *Remember:* Can you recall the definition for _____? What are five words and definitions you have learned today?
- *Understand:* Using your own words, please define _____. How could you rephrase the definition for the word _____?
- *Apply:* Can you explain how these words relate to the topic of _____?
- *Analyze:* How is _____ similar to _____? What is the difference between _____ and _____?

- *Evaluate:* Which words are the most important to the lesson objectives?

## Benefits

- Can be done individually, with a small group, or with the whole class
- Requires only moderate advance preparation from the teacher
- Encourages collaboration of thought
- Helps in classrooms where students have a wide range of academic ability
- Requires understanding and analyzing
- Teaches a skill good readers must possess
- Applicable for a variety of subjects

## Considerations

- This activity may not be productive for the more advanced students.

## Suggestions for Differentiation

- Allow students to work individually or with a small group.
- Have students display groups of words electronically with pictures and/or illustrations.
- Suggest students make a non-linguistic representation for selected vocabulary words.
- Have students keep a vocabulary notebook of new terms. Students would individually decide which terms to include.
- Have students compete for the lists with the greatest number of correct predicted definitions.

## Technology Adaptation

1. Ask students to use an online dictionary to check answers.
2. Ask students to post words, predicted definitions, and context clues on a class blog. Direct students to comment on predictions.

3. Combine student lists and post electronically. Invite students to continue to add to the listing throughout the instructional unit.

**Teacher Notes**

_____

_____

_____

_____

_____

_____

_____

_____

**STRATEGY: LIST, GROUP, LABEL**

**Why Use the List, Group, Label Strategy?**

The purpose of the List, Group, Label Strategy (Taba, 1967) is to assist students in learning new vocabulary by emphasizing word relationships. In addition to helping students understand and remember vocabulary words and phrases, it also supports the activation of background knowledge.

**Types of Texts**

Fiction, Non-Fiction, and Expository Text. This strategy can be easily modified for a variety of content areas.

**Grade Level Adaptability**

Elementary, Secondary, and Post-Secondary.

## Steps in the Process

1. Introduce the selected topic to students.
2. Ask students to brainstorm words related to the topic.
3. Record the words in a manner that can be displayed to everyone.
4. Ask students to individually determine ways the words can be grouped together. Explain they will be asked to share their reasons for the grouping with classmates.
5. Place students in groups of 2–4, and ask them to review the words. They should reach consensus as to how best to place the words into groupings.
6. Instruct students to label each listing of words, and indicate how the words are related.
7. After categories and labels have been assigned, facilitate a class discussion of the terms and words.
8. Direct students to read the assignment.

## Engage with Bloom's Taxonomy

- *Remember:* Using the definition provided within the text, define the word, words, or terms.
- *Understand:* Using your own words, define each word, words, or terms.
- *Apply:* Explain how each term contributes to the overall understanding of the text content.
- *Analyze:* Explain the relationships between the words.
- *Evaluate:* Prioritize the words in relation to their contribution to understanding the instructional objectives. Explain to a classmate how you determined the prioritization.

## Benefits

- Activates background knowledge prior to reading a selection
- Facilitates a deeper understanding of the vocabulary terms
- Engages all students in a classroom for students with a wide range of academic ability

- Provides differentiation through the choice of selected words for each group
- Allows for small group and large group discussion
- Encourages collaboration
- Provides opportunity for students to consider relationships between words
- Can be easily implemented by a substitute teacher
- Easy to implement
- Applicable for a variety of subjects

## Considerations

- If students do not have adequate background knowledge, they may find it difficult to generate a listing of related terms or phrases.

## Suggestions for Differentiation

- Allow students to choose whether to work individually or with a small group.
- Suggest students choose a word map, web, chart, or diagram to display words and categories of words.

## Technology Adaptation

1. Ask each group to create an electronic presentation of the word groups that will be displayed during a whole class discussion.
2. Post categories and words on a class blog.
3. Share the word listings through Twitter.
4. Use an electronic thesaurus or dictionary to add to the listing of words.

## Teacher Notes

_____

_____

_____

_____

_____

_____

_____

_____

_____

## STRATEGY: MAGIC SQUARE

### Why Use the Magic Square Strategy?

The Magic Square Strategy (Vacca and Vacca, 2008) is designed to help reinforce the learning of words and their meanings.

### Types of Texts

Fiction, Non-Fiction, and Expository Text. This strategy can be easily modified for a variety of content areas.

### Grade Level Adaptability

Elementary.

### Steps in the Process

1. Choose vocabulary words from the text.
2. Locate a magic square template on the Internet. (These are plentiful and directions are easily followed.)
3. Ask students to complete the Magic Square.

### Engage with Bloom's Taxonomy

- _Remember:_ Match the definition to word.
- _Understand:_ Ask students to create a Magic Square by putting definitions into their own words.

- *Apply:* How do these words in the Magic Square relate to the overall content of the chapter?
- *Analyze:* How are the words related to each other? Do they have similar prefixes, suffixes, or root words?
- *Evaluate:* Ask students to create their own Magic Square for classmates to complete. Ask them to justify the words chosen.

## Benefits

- Can be done individually or with a small group
- Can be easily implemented by a substitute teacher
- Facilitates differentiation depending on words provided to students
- Makes a novel activity
- Makes a good activity for test review

## Considerations

- This strategy may be too time consuming to do with all vocabulary words.

## Suggestions for Differentiation

- Provide different words or vary the number of vocabulary words.
- Allow some students to work individually while others work with peers.
- Ask students to provide a non-linguistic representation rather than a definition.

## Technology Adaptation

1. Have students create the Magic Square electronically.
2. Encourage the use of an electronic dictionary or thesaurus.
3. Use classroom blogs to give feedback to students related to the choice of words and complexity of chosen words.

## Teacher Notes

_____

_____

_____

_____

_____

_____

_____

_____

## STRATEGY: PREDICTIONS, DEFINITIONS, AND CONNECTIONS

### Why Use the Predictions, Definitions, and Connections Strategy?

The purpose of the Predictions, Definitions, and Connections Strategy (Lenski, Wham, Johns, and Caskey, 2007) is to help students identify unfamiliar words as well as to predict the definition of the term and the connection to the text.

### Types of Texts

Fiction, Non-Fiction, and Expository Text. This strategy can be easily modified for a variety of content areas.

### Grade Level Adaptability

Elementary and Secondary

### Steps in the Process

1. Identify a key term or concept from the reading selection that may be unfamiliar to students.

2. Ask students to write the following on paper:
   - Unfamiliar Word
   - Sentence Containing Unfamiliar Word
   - Predicted Definition Based on Sentence Context
   - Definition of Term
   - Connection to Content
   - Personal Connection
3. Ask students to fill in the sections "Unfamiliar Word," "Sentence Containing Unfamiliar Word," and "Predicted Definition Based on Sentence Context."
4. Using a glossary or dictionary, ask students to write the definition.
5. Have students collaborate and share their ideas.
6. Ask students to work in small groups to complete the remaining parts of the form.

## Engage with Bloom's Taxonomy

- *Remember:* What is the meaning of _____? List five of the previously unknown words and write a definition of the terms.
- *Understand:* Give an example of a _____. Using your own words, restate the definition.
- *Apply:* How does knowing this term or terms help you understand the lesson objectives? How could you classify the words by placing them into groups? How would you label the groups?
- *Analyze:* How are the following words similar? How are they different?
- *Evaluate:* How would you prioritize the words related to their importance in understanding the topic?

## Benefits

- Can be used as a pre-reading or post-reading activity
- Requires active participation from the reader
- Requires only moderate advance preparation from the teacher
- Works one on one, with small groups, and with the whole class

## Considerations

- This strategy may slow the reading of advanced readers.
- This strategy may be too time consuming.

## Suggestions for Differentiation

- Choose words of varying complexity for student groups.
- Allow students to work individually or with a small group.
- Display groups of words electronically with pictures and/or illustrations.
- Display groups of words on paper including a non-linguistic representation.
- Have students keep a vocabulary notebook of new terms. Students individually decide which terms to include.

## Technology Adaptation

1. Using an online dictionary or thesaurus, have students verify definitions.
2. Ask students to find images online that would be a representation of select words.
3. Make the graphic organizer electronically and post it on Glogster.

## Teacher Notes

_____

_____

_____

_____

_____

_____

_____

_____

## STRATEGY: THE ROOT OF THE PROBLEM

### Why Use The Root of the Problem Strategy?

The purpose of The Root of the Problem Strategy is to help students recognize and use root words, prefixes, and suffixes to help decode and determine the meaning of words in print.

### Types of Texts

Fiction, Non-Fiction, and Expository Text. This strategy can be easily modified for a variety of content areas.

### Grade Level Adaptability

Elementary and Secondary

### Steps in the Process

1.  Identify key vocabulary words.
2.  Ask students to research the meaning of each word by paying particular attention to root words, prefixes, and suffixes.
3.  Ask students to compare and contrast the root word meanings with a classmate.
4.  Facilitate a whole class discussion of words and word parts.
5.  Ask students to use parts of words and create new words.
6.  Discuss newly created words with the whole class.

### Engage with Bloom's Taxonomy

- *Remember:* What is the meaning of _____? List five of the previously unknown words and write a definition of the terms.
- *Understand:* Give an example of a _____. Using your own words, restate the definition.
- *Apply:* How does knowing this term or terms help you understand the lesson objectives? Classify the words by placing them into groups. How would you label the groups?
- *Analyze:* How are the following words similar? How are they different?

- *Evaluate:* How would you prioritize the words related to their importance in understanding the topic?

## Benefits

- Can be used as a pre-reading or post-reading activity
- Requires active participation from students
- Requires only moderate advance preparation from the teacher
- Provides for thinking aloud as students discuss how answers were formulated
- Helps students learn how to use structural analysis to support their reading comprehension

## Considerations

- This strategy may be too time consuming.

## Suggestions for Differentiation

- Vary the words provided to them, depending on students' reading level.
- Have students rotate into different groups throughout the lesson.
- Ask students to design a non-linguistic representation of selected words.
- Provide some student groups with examples of newly created words.

## Technology Adaptation

1. Use an online dictionary or thesaurus.
2. Post words on class blog and ask students to respond.
3. Use Wordle for a display of words.

## Teacher Notes

_____

_____

_____

_____

_____

_____

_____

_____

_____

## STRATEGY: THINK ALOUD WITH A TWIST

### Why Use the Think Aloud with a Twist Strategy?

The purpose of the Think Aloud with a Twist Strategy is to assist students as they use visual imagery as a strategy for comprehending text.

### Types of Texts

Fiction, Non-Fiction, and Expository Text. This strategy can be easily modified for a variety of content areas.

### Grade Level Adaptability

Elementary, Secondary, and Post-Secondary.

### Steps in the Process

1. Select a passage that has an accompanying non-linguistic representation.
2. Show students the graphic without the written text and ask them to describe what they see.
3. Direct students to share with others their ideas and responses to the visual image.
4. Encourage students to make predictions of what they believe will be included in the text.

5. Read a portion of the text aloud to the students and ask them to verify predictions.
6. Ask students to identify important vocabulary words from the text, paying particular attention to vocabulary that might be associated with the previously displayed visual image.
7. Ask students to draw a non-linguistic representation of the selected vocabulary words.

## Engage with Bloom's Taxonomy

- *Remember:* What is the meaning of _____? List five of the previously unknown words and write a definition of the terms.
- *Understand:* Give an example of a _____. Using your own words, restate the definition.
- *Apply:* How does knowing this term or terms help you understand the lesson objectives? Classify the words by placing them into groups. How would you label the groups?
- *Analyze:* Compare and contrast the words as they relate to the non-linguistic representation. Explain the process used to select the words more closely related to the visual image.
- *Evaluate:* Review the words selected by classmates. Provide constructive feedback to classmates as to how well their selected words related to the visual representation.

## Benefits

- Can be used as a pre-reading activity
- Requires active participation from the reader
- Requires only moderate advance preparation from the teacher
- Provides for purposeful discussion as students discuss how answers were formulated
- Works one on one, with small groups, and with the whole class
- Requires students to use higher order thinking skills
- Most texts have visual images directly related to the written content
- Provides a novel way of teaching students the value of text graphics

## Considerations

- Student selected words may not necessarily represent all of the important vocabulary words

## Suggestions for Differentiation

- Provide different visual images to groups of students.
- Have students rotate into different groups throughout the lesson.
- Use leveled reading materials.
- Ask students to design a different visual representation.
- Ask students to design a word web representing the visual image.

## Technology Adaptation

1. Display the non-linguistic representation electronically, and ask students to use class blogs or Twitter to share ideas about the visual image.
2. Ask students to locate similar visual images online for the purpose of comparing and contrasting the content with the original images.

## Teacher Notes

_____

_____

_____

_____

_____

_____

_____

_____

## STRATEGY: VOCABULARY CHART

### Why Use the Vocabulary Chart Strategy?

The Vocabulary Chart Strategy (Brunner, 2011) was designed to encourage students to think about vocabulary words they already know and associate the words with a specific topic.

### Types of Texts

Fiction, Non-Fiction, and Expository Text. This strategy can be easily modified for a variety of content areas.

### Grade Level Adaptability

Elementary, Secondary, and Post-Secondary.

### Steps in the Process

1. Introduce the topic of the reading passage to students.
2. Using paper, ask students to divide it vertically into two columns of equal size.
3. At the top of the column on the left, ask students to write the heading "Words I Know." At the top of the column on the right, tell them to write the heading "New Words."
4. Prior to reading the assigned text, ask students to brainstorm vocabulary words they already know related to the topic and record the words in the column on the left (Words I Know).
5. After reading the passage, have students list (in the New Words column) new vocabulary words they encountered in the reading. Direct students to pay particular attention to words in bold or italicized print as well as words contained in captions to a graphic or words within a title or subtitle.
6. Ask students to continue listing terms until they have written several new words.
7. Ask students to work individually or in small groups to define the new vocabulary words. The definition should include how

and why the words are significant as related to the overall subject of the reading.

## Engage with Bloom's Taxonomy

- *Remember*: What is a _____? What is the definition of _____?
- *Understand:* Using your own words, define _____. Draw a non-linguistic representation of the vocabulary word. What is a synonym for the word _____? Write possible test questions that would require other students to understand the meaning of the vocabulary words.
- *Apply:* What are some examples of the word _____? Write a paragraph using some of the vocabulary words.
- *Analyze:* How do the vocabulary words help you understand the lesson objectives?
- *Evaluate:* After all vocabulary words have been defined, ask students to prioritize the words according to importance within the context of the instructional objectives.

## Benefits

- Can be done individually, with a small group, or with the whole class
- Requires little advance preparation from the teacher
- Provides a ready-made study guide of vocabulary words
- Sets a specific purpose for reading
- Can be easily implemented by a substitute teacher

## Considerations

- If students lack initial background knowledge of the topic, additional discussion may need to occur prior to having them read the text.

## Suggestions for Differentiation

- Allow students to work individually or in small groups.

- Have students keep a vocabulary notebook of new terms. Students would individually decide which terms to include.
- Ask students to provide a non-linguistic representation of selected words.
- Have students teach their selected words to others in the class.
- Ask students to choose five of the most important words and explain to a classmate why the each word was chosen.

## Technology Adaptation

1. Ask students to make a chart electronically using graphics, clip art, or symbols.
2. Use Wordle to make a visual display of the words.

## Teacher Notes

_____

_____

_____

_____

_____

_____

_____

_____

_____

## STRATEGY: WORD EXPLORATION

## Why Use Word Exploration Strategy?

The purpose of the Word Exploration Strategy (Vacca and Vacca, 2008) is to help students make connections between words and their prior knowledge.

## Types of Texts

Fiction, Non-Fiction, and Expository Text. This strategy can be easily modified for a variety of content areas.

## Grade Level Adaptability

Elementary, Secondary, and Post-Secondary.

## Steps in the Process

1. Introduce selected vocabulary words or terminology.
2. Invite students to write spontaneously for three to five minutes related to what they already know about the word, words, or phrase. Since students are not writing for an audience, grammar, spelling, and punctuation should not be important.
3. Ask students to share what they have written with others.
4. Help students see similarities and differences related to preconceived ideas about words or terms.

## Engage with Bloom's Taxonomy

- *Remember:* What is the meaning of _____?
- *Understand:* Give an example of a _____.
- *Apply:* What questions do you have about the term _____? What do you hope to learn during this instructional unit?
- *Analyze:* Review the writing of a classmate. Compare and contrast the thoughts of each author.
- *Evaluate:* Compare what you wrote to what is in the text. Based on your current understanding of the topic, how might you modify your free-write?

## Benefits

- Can be used as a pre-reading or post-reading activity
- Activates background knowledge
- Requires only moderate advance preparation from the teacher

- Can be easily implemented by a substitute teacher
- Encourages students to put thoughts into writing
- Works one on one, with small groups, and with the whole class
- Encourages peer-to-peer discussion

## Considerations

- If students lack background knowledge of the topic, this activity may not be productive.

## Suggestions for Differentiation

- Use flexible grouping.
- Vary the vocabulary words.
- Ask students to make a non-linguistic representation of selected words.

## Technology Adaptation

1. Ask students to succinctly communicate thoughts through the use of Twitter.
2. Ask students to post writing on class blog.
3. Use Edmodo to share student writing. Ask students to respond to classmates related to content.

## Teacher Notes

_____

_____

_____

_____

_____

_____

_____

_____

## STRATEGY: WORD QUESTIONING

### Why Use the Word Questioning Strategy?

The purpose of the Word Questioning Strategy (Allen, 1999) is to give students exposure to the meaning of vocabulary words and terms at many levels of Bloom's Taxonomy. The questions provided to students will facilitate a deeper understanding of the vocabulary word or concept.

### Types of Texts

Fiction, Non-Fiction, and Expository Text. This strategy can be easily modified for a variety of content areas.

### Grade Level Adaptability

Elementary, Secondary, and Post-Secondary.

### Steps in the Process

1. Ask students to write the following on a sheet of paper.
   - What is a sentence using the word? (Remember)
   - What are the parts of the word I recognize? (Analyze)
   - What does the word mean? (Understand)
   - What is an example for the word? (Understand)
   - How does the word go with other words or concepts I know? (Apply)
   - What might I be reading about when I find this word? (Apply)
   - Why is this word important for me to know? (Evaluate)
2. Provide the selected vocabulary words to the students and ask them to locate the word in the reading passage.
3. Ask students to write the sentence with the vocabulary terms on the appropriate part of the paper, and direct them to continue to answer the questions from the paper.

### Engage with Bloom's Taxonomy

- See *Steps in the Process*

## Benefits

- Takes little teacher preparation
- Straightforward and easy to explain and understand
- Requires students to think beyond the text
- Can be done individually or in small groups
- Symbols or visual images can be used to answer the questions
- Promotes a deeper understanding of the meaning of the vocabulary words

## Considerations

- If students lack background knowledge, the strategy may not be effective.

## Suggestions for Differentiation

- Choose words of varying complexity for student groups.
- Allow students to work individually or with a small group.
- Display groups of words electronically with pictures and/or illustrations.
- Display groups of words on paper including a non-linguistic representation.
- Have students keep a vocabulary notebook of new terms. Students individually decide which terms to include.

## Technology Adaptation

1. In a computer lab, display different questions on each computer. Have students rotate through the lab answering one question on each computer. At the end of the session, place one or more students at each computer and ask them to share what was listed.

## Teacher Notes

_____

_____

_____

_____

_____

_____

_____

_____

## STRATEGY: WORD SORTS

### Why Use the Word Sorts Strategy?

The purpose of the Word Sorts Strategy (Gillet and Kita, 1979) is to help students organize words based on prior knowledge. A closed word sort requires the teacher to predetermine the categories for the words. An open word sort does not have predetermined categories.

### Types of Texts

Fiction, Non-Fiction, and Expository Text. This strategy can be easily modified for a variety of content areas.

### Grade Level Adaptability

Elementary, Secondary, and Post-Secondary.

### Steps in the Process

1. Select vocabulary words from selected reading.
2. Write the words on note cards, white board, or overhead transparency.
3. Place students into groups of 2-4, and explain they are to sort words according to pre-established categories. (Closed Word Sort)

4. Place students into groups of 2–4 and explain they are to review words and group them according to a category they believe appropriate. (Open Word Sort)
5. After groups have completed the activity, ask them to share their ideas with the whole class.

## Engage with Bloom's Taxonomy

- *Remember*: Using the definition provided within the text, define the word, words, or terms.
- *Understand*: Using your own words, define each word, words, or terms.
- *Apply*: Explain how each term contributes to the overall understanding of the text content.
- *Analyze*: How are the words related to each other?
- *Evaluate*: Prioritize the words in relation to their contribution to understanding the instructional objective. Explain to a classmate how you determined the prioritization.

## Benefits

- Can be easily implemented
- Requires only moderate advance preparation from the teacher
- Positive student attitude toward strategy
- Encourages cooperation among classmates
- Helps in classroom with students having a wide range of academic ability
- Provides a framework for discussion of vocabulary words
- Facilitates a deeper understanding of the vocabulary words
- Provides for differentiation and teacher flexibility depending on selected words and use of closed or open word sort

## Considerations

- None noted.

## Suggestions for Differentiation

- Provide a variety of words or terms, depending on students' reading level.
- Allow students to choose whether to work individually or with a small group.
- Suggest students choose a word map, web, chart, or diagram to display words and categories of words.

## Technology Adaptation

1. Project words electronically, and ask students to create an electronic display of the categories and words.
2. Use an electronic thesaurus or dictionary to add to the listing of words.
3. Post categories and words on class blog.
4. Share the listing through Twitter or a class blog.

## Teacher Notes

_____
_____
_____
_____
_____
_____
_____
_____

## STRATEGY: WORD STUDY

## Why Use Word Study Strategy?

The purpose of the Word Study Strategy (Allen, 2007) is to help students learn to use context clues.

## Types of Texts

Fiction, Non-Fiction, and Expository Text. This strategy can be easily modified for a variety of content areas.

## Grade Level Adaptability

Elementary, Secondary, and Post-Secondary.

## Steps in the Process

1. Select words or phrases from the text.
2. Explain local context—using the words in the sentence to predict meaning.
3. Explain global context—using a larger portion of the text to make predictions.
4. Explain structural analysis—using word part (root words, prefixes, suffixes) to predict the meaning of words.
5. Ask students to work individually or in groups to predict possible meanings for the words or phrases.
6. After predictions are made, provide text to students and have them read the passage that includes the words and phrases.

## Engage with Bloom's Taxonomy

- *Remember:* What is the meaning of _____?
- *Understand:* Give an example of a _____. Restate the definition in your own words.
- *Apply:* What questions do you have about the term _____? What do you hope to learn during this instructional unit? If you used structural analysis to predict the meaning, what clues helped you the most?
- *Analyze:* Review the predictions of a classmate. Compare and contrast these predictions with your own predictions.
- *Evaluate:* Review the predictions of a classmate. Look for differences and convince the classmate that your predictions are more accurate. Justify your answers with concrete evidence and examples.

## Benefits

- Can be used as a pre-reading activity
- Activates background knowledge
- Requires only moderate advance preparation from the teacher
- Can be easily implemented by a substitute teacher
- Works one on one, with small groups, and with the whole class
- Encourages peer-to-peer discussion

## Considerations

- If students lack background knowledge of the topic, this activity may not be productive.

## Suggestions for Differentiation

- Vary vocabulary words based upon complexity and difficulty of text
- Allow students to work individually or in small groups
- Provide a variety of ways for students to display the words and definitions for review (bulletin board display, flash cards, etc.)

## Technology Adaptation

1. Ask students to post predictions on class blog.
2. Use Edmodo to share student predictions. Ask students to respond to classmates about the content.

## Teacher Notes

_____

_____

_____

_____

_____

_____

_____

_____

_____

_____

_____

## STRATEGY: WORD WALL WITH PIZAZZ

### Why Use Word Wall with Pizazz Strategy?

The purpose of the Word Wall with Pizazz Strategy is to help students make connections through the use of visualization.

### Types of Texts

Fiction, Non-Fiction, and Expository Text. This strategy can be easily modified for a variety of content areas.

### Grade Level Adaptability

Elementary and Secondary

### Steps in the Process

1. Select important vocabulary words with emphasis on the ones most essential to student understanding of the instructional content.
2. Present the words in context to the students.
3. Ask students to create a visual display area for the vocabulary words with emphasis on a visually pleasing and creative display surface.
4. Have students write individual words on cards including a definition, use of the word in a sentence, and a non-linguistic representation.
5. Place the vocabulary cards in an organized display.

## Engage with Bloom's Taxonomy

- *Remember:* What is the meaning of _____?
- *Understand:* Give an example of a _____.
- *Apply:* What questions do you have about the term _____? What do you hope to learn during this instructional unit?
- *Analyze:* Group the words in a manner that communicates understanding of the term. Make a visual image that communicates how words are related and connected to the overall instructional objective.
- *Evaluate:* Display the words on the wall in a manner that communicates a hierarchical order.

## Benefits

- Can be used as a pre-reading or post-reading activity
- Provides a novel way of reinforcing words or terminology
- Requires only moderate advance preparation from the teacher
- Facilitates learning of relationships between words
- Works one on one, with small groups, and with the whole class
- Encourages peer-to-peer discussion

## Considerations

- This strategy may be too time consuming to use with all vocabulary words.

## Suggestions for Differentiation

- Provide words of varying complexity and difficulty
- Have selected students work in small groups
- Assign specific tasks within a group (one student write definitions, one student draw a non-linguistic representation of the word, etc.)
- Allow students to choose between an electronic word wall posted on a class website or a more traditional word wall to be posted on a classroom bulletin board

## Technology Adaptation

1.  Ask students to evaluate word wall and post thoughts on a class blog.
2.  Create an electronic word wall.
3.  Use an electronic dictionary or thesaurus to verify definitions.
4.  Use electronic visual images as the non-linguistic representation of selected terms.
5.  Use Wordle to create an electronic visual display of the words.

## Teacher Notes

# 2

# COMPREHENSION

Reading comprehension is the *reason* for reading. It is as simple—and as complicated—as that. If students are to be academically successful in the twenty-first century, they will have to be able to read, reflect, and find the deeper meaning within the text.

Non-fiction and technical textbooks are challenging, and teachers must be ready to provide the necessary support to facilitate learning and ensure student understanding. Reading is not a passive activity, and all must help to ensure it is never reduced to such. As a result, it is imperative for teachers to use the reading methods described within this text routinely and with purpose. Classrooms are filled with diverse learners, and everyone must be ready with a variety of teaching techniques that differentiate instruction and engage students of all backgrounds and abilities.

According to Randall J. Ryder and Michael F. Graves in their 2003 book *Reading and Learning in Content Areas*, "Active reading requires the reader to have a purpose for reading, to activate available knowledge that is related to that purpose, to read for additional information, and, finally, to restructure knowledge by accommodating the new information." Regardless of grade level or content area, most elementary, secondary, and post-secondary students will benefit from direct instruction that supports reading comprehension.

The teaching activities included in this chapter were carefully selected for their ease of use and their ability to actively engage students in the reading process. Each is designed to encourage remembering, understanding, and critical thinking related to difficult text. Most strategies will stretch students to the highest levels of Bloom's Taxonomy, and all will require thoughtful consideration resulting in a greater understanding of content material. Each strategy is explained as first described in the original research; however, a few of the procedures have been modified as a result of feedback from teachers, students, or author experience.

## STRATEGY: AGREE OR DISAGREE

### Why Use the Agree or Disagree Strategy?

The purpose of the Agree or Disagree Strategy (Rasinski and Padak, 1996) is to provide a framework for students to use when sharing their thoughts about multi-faceted issues. This technique encourages critical and complex thinking.

### Types of Texts

Fiction, Non-Fiction, and Expository Text. This strategy can be easily modified for a variety of content areas.

### Grade Level Adaptability

Elementary, Secondary, and Post-Secondary.

### Steps in the Process

1. Formulate several questions related to the reading that reflect varying points of view.
2. Provide questions to the students.
3. After students have read or listened to the selected reading, ask them to write whether they agree or disagree with each statement. Their written statements should include an explanation of why they believe as they do about the topic.

4. After statements are written, discuss with students how they should conduct themselves during a discussion that will include a variety of viewpoints. This would include such things as only one person speaks at a time, participants should remain respectful, all should be allowed to speak and share opinions, etc.

5. Divide students into groups of 3–4, directing group members to discuss each statement and decide if they agree or disagree. One group member should take notes during the discussion and serve as recorder. These notes should include the reasoning behind the opinions expressed by individuals and/or the group.

6. When the small groups have completed their assignment, facilitate a discussion of the statements with the whole class.

7. When discussions are complete, ask students to get into groups based on their preferred opinions.

8. Compare the groups and discuss whether opinions changed as a result of the reading or class discussion.

## Engage with Bloom's Taxonomy

- *Remember:* What are three things you want to remember from what you read?
- *Understand:* Using your own words, summarize what you read.
- *Apply:* What information from the reading would you use to justify your position?
- *Analyze:* Compare and contrast your opinion to those of your classmates.
- *Evaluate:* Are the differences of opinions expressed by agreeing or disagreeing with the statements supported by the evidence? Be specific. After listening to other points of view, defend or modify your original opinion.

## Benefits

- Provides a framework for students when reading difficult and challenging material

- Provides teacher flexibility and the opportunity to differenti-ate instruction depending on the content of the questions given to each group
- Facilitates a deeper understanding of the text
- Actively engages students in the process of reading and deliberation
- Encourages students to see more than one side of an issue
- Facilitates better preparation for reading expository material as an independent reader
- Provides a constructive opportunity for "arguing" and defend-ing a variety of points of view
- Provides a framework for a civil and respectful discussion
- Facilitates retention through in-depth discussion

## Considerations

- Students may be tempted to become too emotional defending a point of view.
- Teacher preparation time is needed to formulate engaging and thought-provoking questions and statements.
- Teachers may need to spend preparatory time explaining the appropriate way to discuss a variety of perspectives in a civil manner.
- Not all text material provides a variety of reader perspectives.
- Teachers will need strong classroom management skills.

## Suggestions for Differentiation

- Provide statements of varying complexity.
- Group students based on topic interest.
- Limit the scope of the assignment.
- Provide varying levels of activating background knowledge.

## Technology Adaptation

1. Ask students to explore alternative positions by researching the topic on the Internet. Students should be prepared to

agree or disagree with new information and be prepared to explain what changed their opinions.

2. Email statements to students and ask them to respond electronically.

3. Using Diigo, ask students to analyze and organize additional research on the topic.

4. Using Twitter, instruct students to justify a position using 140 characters or less.

## Teacher Notes

_____

_____

_____

_____

_____

_____

_____

_____

## STRATEGY: ANTICIPATION GUIDE

### Why Use the Anticipation Guide Procedure?

The Anticipation Guide Procedure (Vacca and Vacca, 1989) was developed to encourage students to consider thoughts and opinions about topics in order to activate background knowledge and peak interest in the reading selection.

### Types of Texts

Fiction, Non-Fiction, and Expository Text. This strategy can be easily modified for a variety of content areas.

## Grade Level Adaptability

Elementary, Secondary, and Post-Secondary.

## Steps in the Process

1. Read the text and develop anticipatory statements. These statements should be brief and declarative.
2. Put the statements in a format that encourages anticipation and prediction.
3. Prior to asking students to read the text, ask them to consider the statements and respond verbally or in writing.
4. Assign the text.
5. Ask students to evaluate the statements according to the author's intent and purpose.
6. Tell students to compare their predictions and pre-reading thoughts to the author's intended meaning.

## Engage with Bloom's Taxonomy

- *Remember*: What are five important details from the reading selection?
- *Understand:* What do you want to remember? Why do you believe it is important to remember?
- *Apply:* How can you use the information from the reading selection to support what you already know about the topic?
- *Analyze*: What other statements could have been included in the Anticipation Guide?
- *Evaluate*: Critique the statements on the Anticipation Guide. Which ones helped you the most in terms of remembering and understanding what was read?

## Benefits

- Can be done individually, with a small group, or with the whole class
- Provides a novel method of activating background knowledge
- Sets a specific purpose for reading

## Considerations

- If students lack initial background knowledge of the topic, additional discussion will need to occur prior to having them read the text.
- It may be too time consuming to develop the Anticipation Guide statements.

## Suggestions for Differentiation

- Allow for flexible grouping.
- Adjust the amount of information for activation of background knowledge.
- Allow students to share information among groups and with individuals.

## Technology Adaptation

1. Tell students to research the topic on the Internet as a pre- or post-reading activity.
2. Ask them to record the information on a class blog.
3. Use Google Docs to display the Anticipation Guide questions and statements.

## Teacher Notes

_____

_____

_____

_____

_____

_____

_____

_____

## STRATEGY: ATTRIBUTE WEB

### Why Use the Attribute Web Strategy?

The purpose of the Attribute Web Strategy (Lenski, Wham, Johns, and Caskey, 2007) is to provide students the opportunity to analyze a character from a text and construct a visual representation of that individual. This activity provides students the opportunity to visualize how a character looks, acts, or feels. The Attribute Web may also include how other characters within the text perceive the individual.

### Types of Texts

Fiction, Non-Fiction, and Expository Text. This strategy can be easily modified for a variety of content areas.

### Grade Level Adaptability

Elementary, Secondary, and Post-Secondary.

### Steps in the Process

1. Discuss the importance of character analysis, including a review of the attributes of a character within the reading. Attributes may include physical characteristics, personality characteristics, or a combination of the two.
2. After reading the selection, ask students to work individually or in small groups to create the Attribute Web.
3. Instruct students to draw a circle in the middle of a piece of paper and place the character's name in the circle.
4. Using the basic web format, ask students to brainstorm what they consider to be significant attributes of the character and include the listing on the web. The attributes may include single words or descriptive phrases.
5. Ask students to share the web with others.

## Engage with Bloom's Taxonomy

- *Remember:* What words are used within the reading selection that would describe a character?
- *Understand:* What synonyms could you use to describe a character?
- *Apply:* Using the words from the Attribute Web, write a descriptive paragraph about the character.
- *Analyze:* Using the Attribute Web, make a flow chart that illustrates the development of the character.
- *Evaluate:* Prepare a scoring rubric for the assignment.

## Benefits

- Provides opportunity for individual work or a collaborative effort
- Encourages attention to detail and student engagement
- Takes little teacher preparation
- Straightforward and easy to explain and understand
- Helps students understand how an author develops a storyline through characterization
- Encourages collaboration
- Provides a purpose for reading
- Can be easily implemented by a substitute teacher
- May be an ongoing activity while book is being read

## Considerations

1. None noted.

## Suggestions for Differentiation

- Allow some students to work individually and others to work with a small group.
- Have selected students develop a scoring rubric for the assignment.

- Allow some students to produce an electronic document while others complete the assignment using paper and pencil.
- Provide some students the descriptive words in advance.
- Have students use symbols, rather than words, to describe the attributes.

## Technology Adaptation

1. Use one of the free word web frameworks available on the Internet. Ask students to select an organizer and create an electronic Attribute Web using sound, color, and animation.
2. Use an electronic thesaurus to locate additional descriptive words.

## Teacher Notes

_____

_____

_____

_____

_____

_____

_____

_____

_____

## STRATEGY: BODY BIOGRAPHIES

### Why Use the Body Biography Strategy?

The Body Biography Strategy (Underwood, 1987) was designed to give students the opportunity to study an individual or group of individuals for the purpose of understanding point of view.

## Types of Texts

Fiction, Non-Fiction, and Expository Text. This strategy can be easily modified for a variety of content areas.

## Grade Level Adaptability

Elementary and Secondary.

## Steps in the Process

1. Explain to students that they will be using their creative ability to develop a body biography of a significant person.
2. Ask students to select or be prepared to designate which individual will be researched.
3. Encourage students to use a variety of resources to develop a comprehensive point of view.
4. Tell students they should make a listing of the characteristics, events, people, places, things, etc., that might "define" this individual.
5. After students have done the necessary research, tell them to draw a basic outline of a person on a large piece of paper.
6. Using the list of information, ask students to determine the best way to represent his or her information on the body figure.
7. Encourage students to use symbols, rather than words, to depict important information on the body.
8. Display the bodies throughout the room and encourage students to provide feedback to classmates.
9. Ask students to guess whom each body biography represents.

## Engage with Bloom's Taxonomy

- *Remember:* Who was this individual?
- *Understand:* Summarize why this individual is significant.
- *Apply:* Explain how the visual images on the "body" reflect the individual.
- *Analyze:* Why did you choose those specific images, and why are they important to this "body"?

- *Evaluate:* Critique the body biographies of classmates, and provide constructive feedback.

## Benefits

- Requires active participation from the reader
- Requires only moderate advance preparation from the teacher
- Encourages positive student attitudes toward strategy
- Encourages research with a purpose
- Helps in classroom with students having a wide range of academic ability
- Makes a novel activity

## Considerations

- This strategy may be too time consuming.
- Large sheets of paper with markers must be purchased in advance.
- A model or example should be developed in advance.

## Suggestions for Differentiation

- Use leveled text for research.
- Use flexible groups.
- Allow for variation of final product.
- Ask some students to develop opposing biographies of an individual.

## Technology Adaptation

1. Suggest students use only electronic images to create the body biographies.
2. Use Google Docs to create the images for sharing.
3. Use Diigo to bookmark information for researching an individual.
4. Use Animoto to allow for a video creation of a body biography.
5. Use Teacher Tube to provide a way for students to "present" their "body" to classmates.

## Teacher Notes

_____

_____

_____

_____

_____

_____

_____

_____

_____

## STRATEGY: BRAINSTORMING

### Why Use the Brainstorming Strategy?

The purpose of the Brainstorming Strategy (Vacca and Vacca, 1989) is to allow students the opportunity to mentally engage and share their knowledge and experiences prior to reading the text.

### Types of Texts

Fiction, Non-Fiction, and Expository Text. This strategy can be easily modified for a variety of content areas.

### Grade Level Adaptability

Elementary, Secondary, and Post-Secondary.

### Steps in the Process

1. Display a listing of vocabulary words and important concepts from the reading.
2. Ask students to identify what they already know about the words. This can be done in writing or verbally.

3. Facilitate a whole class discussion related to the topic and selected words.
4. Tell students to read the text for the purpose of expanding on what they already know.
5. After students have read the reading selection, ask them to share with a partner, small group, or the whole class what they learned from the reading.

## Engage with Bloom's Taxonomy

- *Remember:* What do you recall from the reading?
- *Understand:* Rephrase some of the author's statements.
- *Apply:* Locate and explain examples from the text of the vocabulary words.
- *Analyze:* How is the new information you learned connected to what you already knew?
- *Evaluate:* What is the value of learning and understanding the text content? In what ways is the information relevant?

## Benefits

- Provides structure for students when reading difficult and challenging material
- Provides teacher the opportunity to pre-teach key vocabulary
- Actively engages readers in the reading process
- Can be easily implemented by a substitute teacher
- Easy to implement
- Applicable for a variety of subjects

## Considerations

- If students do not have adequate background knowledge, they may find this activity too difficult.

## Suggestions for Differentiation

- Provide graphic organizers.
- Use flexible grouping.

- Pre-assess knowledge to determine the need to activate background knowledge.
- Use reading buddies.
- Use different words with different groups of students.
- Use non-linguistic representations for vocabulary words.
- Use visual aids such as graphs, charts, or pictures.

## Technology Adaptation

1. Use Google Docs to create a graphic organizer with the terms and concepts for the class to use as a study guide.
2. Use Glogster to create a virtual poster of the lesson content.

## Teacher Notes

_____

_____

_____

_____

_____

_____

_____

_____

_____

## STRATEGY: CHARACTER QUOTES

### Why Use the Character Quotes Strategy?

The purpose of the Character Quotes Strategy (Buehl, 2001) is to motivate students to read the assigned text, as well as to help them analyze and predict character traits of an individual in the upcoming reading selection. This activity is an engaging "set" to a lesson when students are expected to read about an individual or individuals.

## Types of Texts

Fiction, Non-Fiction, and Expository Text. This strategy can be easily modified for a variety of content areas. It is especially effective with biographies, autobiographies, or any text that includes quotations from a historical figure.

## Grade Level Adaptability

Elementary, Secondary, and Post-Secondary.

## Steps in the Process

1. Preview the text for the purpose of finding quotes from a character that provide insight into the individual's personality.
2. Tell students all quotes are from the same character.
3. Write quotes on individual pieces of paper for distribution to student groups.
4. Divide students into groups of 3–4 and give each group 1–3 quotes.
5. Instruct students to make predictions based on the quotations related to the personality of the character. Encourage them to generate as many words or descriptors as possible.
6. When all groups have completed the assignment, ask one individual from each group to read the quotation and descriptors to the class. For the purpose of comparison, these traits should be recorded on a transparency or marker board.
7. Encourage discussion as to what was stated in the quotation that gave clues or hints related to personality traits.
8. Tell students to read the text for the purpose of determining if predictions were accurate.
9. If time allows, ask students to write a personality profile of the character. Tell them they may be asked to read the profile to the class.

## Engage with Bloom's Taxonomy

- *Remember:* Restate the quote to others within the group.
- *Understand:* What is the main idea of this quote?

- *Apply*: Using information from the quote, write a descriptive paragraph about the character.
- *Analyze:* Compare and contrast quotes with another group.
- *Evaluate:* In determining the identity of the speaker, which quote was most helpful? Be prepared to justify your answers.

## Benefits

- Enhances reading by making predictions
- Provides positive interaction with peers
- Activates background knowledge
- Facilitates a deeper understanding of the text, as well as a character within the text
- Engages all students in a classroom with a wide range of academic ability
- Provides differentiation through the choice of selected quotations for each group
- Allows for both small group and large group discussion
- Encourages critical thinking

## Considerations

- Initial teacher preparation may take time due to the importance of locating insightful and appropriate character quotations.

## Suggestions for Differentiation

- Provide quotes of varying complexity.
- Use flexible student groups.

## Technology Adaptation

1. After students know the name of the character or individual, ask them to use the Internet to locate information related to how others might have described the individual. Have students compare or contrast different perspectives.
2. Use a computer lab to display a different quote on each computer. Have students move around the room and list

character traits related to the displayed quote. After students have rotated through the room, assign each student to a computer and have him read the quote and what was recorded to the class.

## Teacher Notes

_____

_____

_____

_____

_____

_____

_____

_____

## STRATEGY: DIRECTED READING THINKING ACTIVITY (DRTA)

### Why Use the DRTA Strategy?

The purpose of the DRTA Strategy (Stauffer, 1976) is to help students read critically and reflect on what they read. This strategy helps students determine a purpose for reading, carefully examine the text, and remain engaged throughout the lesson. Although this strategy can be modified for non-fiction (Content Directed Thinking Activity), it is easily implemented with fiction.

The teacher uses three basic questions. What do you think is going to happen? Why do you think so? Can you prove it?

### Types of Texts

Fiction, Non-Fiction, and Expository Text. This strategy can be easily modified for a variety of content areas.

## Grade Level Adaptability

Elementary, Secondary, and Post-Secondary.

## Steps in the Process

1. Read the selection to select pre-determined stopping points.
2. Tell students they will need a cover sheet.
3. Ask students to cover everything but the title of the selection.
4. Tell students to read the title and make predictions about the story contents.
5. As students make predictions, ask for "evidence" as to why they believe the prediction is correct.
6. Ask students to read a portion of the text to a predetermined stopping point. Tell them they will review their initial predictions, as well as make new predictions based on the reading. Students should use paper to cover text that has not yet been read.
7. After students have finished reading the designated text, ask questions.
8. Fiction—What has happened so far? What do you think is going to happen next? Why do you think so? Can you prove it it?
9. Non-fiction—What do you need to remember about what you read? What do you think the author will discuss in the next section? Why do you think so? What do you consider to be most important from the reading?
10. Continue the process until text selection has been read completely.

## Engage with Bloom's Taxonomy

- *Remember:* List three details from the reading selection.
- *Understand:* What is the main idea of the reading selection?
- *Apply:* What examples from the text can you find that illustrates the information?
- *Analyze:* Why do you think the character responded the way he did?

- *Evaluate:* What information from the text could you use to support a specific point of view?
- *Create:* What would be an alternative ending for the story?

## Benefits

- Easily implemented
- Requires active participation from the reader
- Requires only moderate advance preparation from the teacher
- Can be easily implemented by a substitute teacher
- Encourages positive student attitudes toward strategy
- Encourages silent reading
- Helps in classroom when students have a wide range of academic ability
- Encourages teachers to "think aloud" with students as predictions and answers are formulated
- Works one on one, with small groups, and with the whole class
- Breaks the passage into manageable parts for students and teacher
- Can easily be implemented with non-fiction text

## Considerations

- This strategy may slow the reading of advanced readers.

## Suggestions for Differentiation

- Use leveled reading texts.
- Allow students to select the reading passages based on interest and genre.
- Provide visual aids for some students, e.g., graphs, charts.
- Ask some students to read a graphic organizer, rather than the text.

## Technology Adaptation

1. Ask students to put predictions on a class blog.
2. Ask students to use an electronic poll to rank predictions.

**Teacher Notes**

---
---
---
---
---
---
---
---

## STRATEGY: GRAPHIC NOVEL

### Why Use the Graphic Novel Strategy?

The Graphic Novel Strategy was designed to help express their understanding of the reading content in a manner that supports visual imaging and dialog.

### Types of Texts

Fiction and Non-Fiction Text. This strategy can be easily modified for a variety of content areas.

### Grade Level Adaptability

Elementary and Secondary.

### Steps in the Process

1. Choose passages within a text that are particularly important to the students' overall understanding of the content.
2. Assign individuals or small groups of students parts of the text for reading.

3. Explain that the purpose for reading is to be prepared to make a comic book representation of the content. In other words, students will tell a "story" with pictures and words. NOTE: When explaining this to students initially, provide a variety of comic book prototypes.
4. Tell students to jot down important information from the text that will help them remember important details.
5. After students have read the selection, have them create a comic strip that explains what was read.
6. Ask students to share their comic book creations with classmates.

## Engage with Bloom's Taxonomy

- *Remember:* Recall as much as possible about what was read.
- *Understand:* Identify the most important information from the text.
- *Apply:* What symbols will you use for the comic strip?
- *Analyze:* Explain to classmates how you decided what would be included in the comic strip.
- *Evaluate:* What constructive feedback could you give to a classmate that would improve a comic strip?

## Benefits

- Can be done individually or with a small group
- Sets a specific purpose for reading
- Provides a novel activity
- Helps create visual images of the text

## Considerations

- This strategy may be too time consuming.

## Suggestions for Differentiation

- After completion of the comic strips, photocopy them, cut them into sections, and have students reassemble.

- Have some students provide dialogue while others provide the non-linguistic representations.

## Technology Adaptation

1. Use an electronic comic creator available online.

## Teacher Notes

_____

_____

_____

_____

_____

_____

_____

_____

_____


## STRATEGY: DOUBLE ENTRY JOURNAL

## Why Use the Double Entry Journal Strategy?

The purpose of the Double Entry Journal Strategy (Vacca and Vacca, 2008) is to facilitate students while they read for deeper meaning.

## Types of Texts

Fiction, Non-Fiction, and Expository Text.

## Grade Level Adaptability

Upper Elementary, Secondary, and Post-Secondary.

## Steps in the Process

1. Ask students to divide sheets of notebook paper in half lengthwise.
2. Explain to students that the left column of the journal is to be used to record words, quotes, or passages from the text they believe are relevant to their understanding of the material.
3. Tell students to use the right column to record their reactions, interpretations, and responses to the information recorded in the left column.

NOTE: When students are learning how to use this strategy, it is recommended the teacher provide headings for both columns. For some students, it may work best to put the heading "What is . . . . . .?" over the column on the left and "What does it mean to me?" over the column on the right.

## Engage with Bloom's Taxonomy

- *Remember:* What do you want to remember from the reading?
- *Understand:* Using your own words, summarize the main idea of the text.
- *Apply:* How does the information you read help you understand the overall content?
- *Analyze:* What conclusions can you draw from what you have read?
- *Evaluate:* What information could you use to support a specific point of view from the reading?

## Benefits

- Supports future independent learning
- Helps students read for deeper meaning
- Encourages active and purposeful reading
- Straightforward, easy to explain and understand
- Provides a study guide for future use
- Requires very little teacher preparation time

## Considerations

- Some students may need help deciding labels for each column.

## Suggestions for Differentiation

- Work individually or with a partner.
- Adjust column headings for students depending on background knowledge and ability.
- Have some students use a combination of non-linguistic representations and words.

## Technology Adaptation

1. Create an electronic display of the two column notes to be shared with the class.
2. Use Google Docs to share student notes.

## Teacher Notes

_____

_____

_____

_____

_____

_____

_____

_____

## STRATEGY: FLIP

## Why Use the Flip Strategy?

The Flip Strategy (Fuentes, 1998) was designed to help students assess their own interest in and prior knowledge of a topic before reading the selection.

## Types of Texts

Fiction, Non-Fiction, and Expository Text. This strategy can be easily modified for a variety of content areas.

## Grade Level Adaptability

Elementary, Secondary, and Post-Secondary.

## Steps in the Process

1. Preview the reading selection to determine where students might struggle with understanding. Think of F (Friendliness of Features), L (Language), I (Interest), and P (Prior Knowledge).
2. Discuss with students the friendliness of the features, the language of the text, what makes the text interesting, and what students should already know related to the subject. NOTE: If student interest is not high, find ways to relate the content to what is important to them.
3. Divide the reading into manageable parts and provide questions to help guide the reading of the text.
4. After students have read the text, facilitate small or large group discussion of the content.

## Engage with Bloom's Taxonomy

- *Remember:* List the important points from the text.
- *Understand:* Prioritize the information on the list of what is remembered from the text.
- *Apply:* What examples did the author use to explain the information?
- *Analyze:* Predict what will be included in the remaining text. Be able to explain why you believe these ideas will be included.
- *Evaluate:* What other information would help you to understand the content?

## Benefits

- Easy to remember the steps in the process
- Provides a novel method of introducing the text
- Helpful in classroom with students having a wide range of academic ability
- Can be easily implemented by a substitute teacher
- Supports student independent learning

## Considerations

- This strategy may not be helpful to the most advanced readers.

## Suggestions for Differentiation

- Allow students to work individually or in small groups.
- Use leveled readers.
- Limit the scope of the assignment for some students.

## Technology Adaptation

1. Tell students to research the topic on the Internet to find further information.
2. Ask students to record the information on a class blog.
3. Have students create an electronic word search of important terms.

## Teacher Notes

_____

_____

_____

_____

_____

_____

## STRATEGY: FOUR CORNERS DEBATE

### Why Use the Four Corners Debate Strategy?

The purpose of the Four Corners Debate Strategy (Jonson, 2006) is to facilitate discussion that encourages more than one point of view. It encourages students to consider what was read, express their thoughts, listen to the ideas and opinions of others, and draw their own conclusions.

### Types of Texts

Fiction, Non-Fiction, and Expository Text. This strategy can be easily modified for a variety of content areas.

### Grade Level Adaptability

Upper Elementary, Secondary, and Post-Secondary.

### Steps in the Process

1. Tell students they are going to read a text that may help them develop an opinion about a specific subject.
2. Introduce important vocabulary words.
3. Ask students to make predictions related to what they believe will be included in the text.
4. Post four signs for the room—"Agree," "Disagree," "Strongly Agree," and "Strongly Disagree."
5. Display a statement and ask students to consider whether they agree, disagree, strongly agree, or strongly disagree.
6. Ask students to move to the corner of the room that reflects their opinion.
7. Allow five minutes for each group to discuss their opinions.
8. Ask each group to select a spokesperson for the group.
9. Allow each group to present their respective positions.
10. After discussion and debate, allow students to reconsider and change, or not change, their respective positions.

## Engage with Bloom's Taxonomy

- *Remember:* What do you want to remember from the reading?
- *Understand:* Using your own words, summarize the main idea of the text.
- *Apply:* Explain your position and opinion using vocabulary words from the text.
- *Analyze:* What ideas helped you formulate your opinion?
- *Evaluate:* Which ideas were the most compelling?

## Benefits

- Supports critical thinking
- Helps students read for deeper meaning
- Encourages active and purposeful reading
- Straightforward, easy to explain and understand
- Provides a novel method of interacting with text
- Sets a specific purpose for reading
- Requires students to consider a variety of perspectives
- Encourages interactive learning
- Can be used as a pre- or post-reading activity

## Considerations

- The text should provide information that may be controversial.
- Some students may find it difficult to consider a perspective other than their own.
- Good classroom management skills will be necessary.

## Suggestions for Differentiation

- Provide a variety of reading material.
- Use heterogeneous grouping of students.
- Use listening stations and graphic organizers to share text content.
- Assign specific roles for the debate, e.g., moderator, speaker, note taker.

## Technology Adaptation

1. None noted.

## Teacher Notes

_____

_____

_____

_____

_____

_____

_____

_____

## STRATEGY: GUIDED READING PROCEDURE

### Why Use Guided Reading Procedure Strategy?

The Guided Reading Procedure Strategy (Manzo, 1975) was designed to help students read for detail and reconstruct the author's message.

### Types of Texts

Fiction, Non-Fiction, and Expository Text. This strategy can be easily modified for a variety of content areas.

### Grade Level Adaptability

Elementary, Secondary, and Post-Secondary.

### Steps in the Process

1. Prepare students for reading by clarifying key concepts and determining what they know and what they do not know.

2. Assign the reading selection.
3. After students finish reading, have them turn their books face down and tell what they remember from the reading.
4. Record what students remember with a visual display.
5. Redirect students to the text and have them review their notes. They should make corrections as necessary.
6. Tell students to organize the notes into a format that makes sense, e.g., outline, chronological order.
7. Ask students to summarize what they learned from the reading selection.

## Engage with Bloom's Taxonomy

- *Remember:* List the important points from the reading selection.
- *Understand:* Summarize the main idea from each section of text.
- *Apply:* How can you use these notes to help learn the information?
- *Analyze:* What inferences can you draw from the reading selection?
- *Evaluate:* Review the guided reading notes for clarity, depth, and breadth. Skim the reading and add or delete as necessary.

## Benefits

- Can be done individually, with a small group, or with the whole class
- Requires little advance preparation from the teacher
- Provides a thorough and comprehensive method for understanding text
- Sets a specific purpose for reading
- Can be easily implemented by a substitute teacher
- May serve as a guide for further study

## Considerations

- Due to the comprehensive nature of the strategy, it may be too time consuming.

## Suggestions for Differentiation

- Use flexible groups.
- Provide teacher-made questions to selected students to help guide the reading.
- Provide a graphic organizer with the text information to some students.

## Technology Adaptation

1. Tell students to research the topic on the Internet to find further information.
2. Ask students to record their notes on a class blog.
3. Ask students to use Google Docs to collaborate with classmates.

## Teacher Notes

_____

_____

_____

_____

_____

_____

_____

_____

## STRATEGY: KNOWLEDGE CHART

## Why Use the Knowledge Chart Strategy?

The Knowledge Chart Strategy (Marzano, 2004) was designed to encourage students to think about what they already know and relate it to what they read from the text. This strategy supports student understanding of the main idea, as well as detailed information, from the text.

## Types of Texts

Fiction, Non-Fiction, and Expository Text.

## Grade Level Adaptability

Elementary, Secondary, and Post-Secondary.

## Steps in the Process

1. Locate a text or visual images to share with students.
2. Give students paper and ask them to divide it vertically into two columns of equal size. The teacher may draw a similar graphic organizer on a marker board.
3. At the top of the column on the left, ask students to write "Prior Knowledge." At the top of the column on the right, ask them to write "New Knowledge."
4. Prior to reading the assigned text, ask students to brainstorm what they already know about the topic and record the information in the column under "Prior Knowledge."
5. After reading the passage, have students list in the "New Knowledge" column information from what they have read. Students should continue until they have listed several pieces of new information.
6. Using the information from both columns, ask students to work individually or in small groups to formulate questions for what they would still like to learn about the topic.

## Engage with Bloom's Taxonomy

- *Remember:* What are five important details from the reading selection?
- *Understand:* What do you want to remember? Why do you believe it is important to remember?
- *Apply:* How can you use the information from the reading selection to solve a problem?
- *Analyze:* Using the information from the reading selection, develop a hypothesis.

- *Evaluate*: Critique the Knowledge Chart of a classmate, and make suggestions for improvement.

## Benefits

- Can be done individually, with a small group, or with the whole class
- Requires little advance preparation from the teacher
- Provides a novel method of activating background knowledge
- Sets a specific purpose for reading
- Helps in classroom where students have a wide range of academic ability
- Requires students to compare and contrast information
- Can be easily implemented by a substitute teacher
- Serves as a study guide

## Considerations

- If students lack initial background knowledge of the topic, additional discussion will need to occur prior to having them read the text.

## Suggestions for Differentiation

- Allow for flexible grouping.
- Adjust the amount of information for activation of background knowledge.
- Allow students to share information among groups and with individuals.
- Give students the choice of using symbols or words for the Knowledge Chart.

## Technology Adaptation

1. Tell students to research the topic on the Internet as a pre- or post-reading activity. Ask them to record the additional information on the Knowledge Chart.

2. Ask students to create the Knowledge Chart electronically using pictures, words, or symbols.
3. Use Google Docs to develop a Knowledge Chart.

**Teacher Notes**

_____

_____

_____

_____

_____

_____

## STRATEGY: LITERATURE CIRCLES

### Why Use the Literature Circles Strategy?

The purpose of the Literature Circles Strategy (Daniels, 1994) is to facilitate student led discussions related to self-selected reading material.

### Types of Texts

Fiction, Non-Fiction, and Expository Text.

### Grade Level Adaptability

Upper Elementary, Secondary, and Post-Secondary.

### Steps in the Process

1. Direct students to choose their own reading selection. It is helpful to designate a genre or several books from which to chose.
2. Assign student groups based on chosen reading material.

3. Encourage students to use sticky notes, highlighting, or other forms of note taking.
4. Tell students they will be participating in small group discussions related to the reading.
5. After students have read to an agreed on chapter in the book, provide class time for discussion of the reading material. Encourage students to make personal connections to the material. As a variation of the strategy, provide sample questions for student consideration. These questions can be provided as a pre- or post-reading part of the strategy.
6. Explain that all students are to participate equally during the discussion. NOTE: The extent of the teacher's role in the group is a professional decision made by the instructor.

## Engage with Bloom's Taxonomy

- *Remember:* What do you want to remember?
- *Understand:* How did you feel about . . .? Summarize what happened when . . .?
- *Apply:* How did the character feel when . . .?
- *Analyze:* How is this book different from others you have read? How is this book similar to others you have read?
- *Evaluate:* As a participant in the Literature Circle, what worked well? What did you learn, and why is it important to learn?

## Benefits

- Allows student choice of reading selection
- Encourages student-initiated discussion
- Engages most students
- Encourages active and purposeful learning
- Straightforward, easy to explain and understand
- Provides novelty
- Can be done as a culminating activity or as a review for a more formal assessment
- Differentiates content based on selection of reading material and sample discussion questions

## Considerations

- The assessment of learning may be challenging.
- The activity may take several class periods to complete.
- Some students may lack personal commitment to the activity.
- Teacher preparation time may increase due to the need for familiarity of reading selections and planning discussions of several texts simultaneously.

## Suggestions for Differentiation

- Assign a genre, but allow students to select the reading material.
- Use flexible grouping.
- Use leveled reading material.
- Allow additional time for some groups to complete the task.
- Provide listening centers for use by some students.

## Technology Adaptation

1. Ask students to utilize classroom blogs to discuss the book's content.
2. As a culminating activity, ask students to create an electronic visual representation of the book to share with the class.

## Teacher Notes

_____

_____

_____

_____

_____

_____

_____

## STRATEGY: NOTE CUE CARDS

### Why Use the Note Cue Cards Strategy?

The Note Cue Cards Strategy (Manzo and Manzo, 1990) was designed to help students identify important information in a text and to facilitate discussion of key terms and concepts after reading is completed.

### Types of Texts

Fiction, Non-Fiction, and Expository Text. This strategy can be easily modified for a variety of content areas.

### Grade Level Adaptability

Elementary, Secondary, and Post-Secondary.

### Steps in the Process

1. Choose a passage that is important for students to understand.
2. Prepare note cards so each student has at least one card. Some cards should have questions. Some cards should have answers, and some cards should have comments about the text.
3. Tell students the cards will help them identify important information from the text.
4. Explain to students that, as they read the text, they should also create their own questions.
5. Distribute note cards to students.
6. Ask students to preview the text, read the cards, and think of how the cards relate to what will be read.
7. Ask a student to read a card with a question, read a card that might answer the question, and then read a comment card that is related.
8. Ask students to read the text.
9. After the reading, distribute more note cards. Students can write their own note cards or use ones supplied by the teacher.

## Engage with Bloom's Taxonomy

- *Remember:* What are five important details from the reading selection?
- *Understand:* What do you want to remember? Why is it important to remember?
- *Apply:* How can you use the information to support what you already know?
- *Analyze:* What other questions could have been included in the Note Cue Cards?
- *Evaluate:* Review the Note Cue Cards of classmates. Give them feedback related to how well the questions, answers, and comments support the overall learning of the content.

## Benefits

- Can be done individually, with a small group, or with the whole class
- Sets a specific purpose for reading
- Provides a novel activity
- Can be individually and teacher directed
- Supports independent learning

## Considerations

- This strategy may be too time consuming.

## Suggestions for Differentiation

- Provide different cards depending on reading ability and background knowledge.
- Use leveled texts.
- Use flexible grouping.
- Pre-teach selected vocabulary words to some students.

## Technology Adaptation

1. Tell students to research the topic on the Internet as they develop their own note card questions, answers, and comments.

2. Use Google Docs to display the note card questions and statements.

**Teacher Notes**

_____

_____

_____

_____

_____

_____

_____

## STRATEGY: OPEN, RECOGNIZE, DRAW, EXPLAIN, AND REUSE (ORDER)

### Why Use the ORDER Strategy?

The purpose of the ORDER Strategy (Bulgren and Scanlon, 1998) is to assist students in visually organizing and reviewing information.

### Types of Texts

Fiction, Non-Fiction, and Expository Text. This strategy can be easily modified for a variety of content areas.

### Grade Level Adaptability

Elementary, Secondary, and Post-Secondary.

### Steps in the Process

1. Tell students this strategy will require them to open their minds and take notes, recognize the structure within the text,

draw an organizer, explain the organizer to others, and reuse the organizer as a study guide.
2. Model how to use the strategy with the text.
3. Ask students to work independently or with a partner for the purpose of developing the study guide.
4. After study guides have been developed, ask students to share with classmates.

## Engage with Bloom's Taxonomy

- *Remember:* What do you want to remember from the reading?
- *Understand:* Explain the main idea from the reading to a classmate.
- *Apply:* Locate the important vocabulary words within the text, and explain the relationships between the words.
- *Analyze:* Organize the information from the text in a manner that makes sense to you.
- *Evaluate:* Assess your knowledge of the topic. What needs clarification and additional information? What do you understand well?

## Benefits

- Supports critical thinking
- Helps students read for deeper meaning
- Encourages active and purposeful reading
- Straightforward, easy to explain and understand
- Provides a novel method of interacting with text
- Sets a specific purpose for reading

## Considerations

- The teacher may need to model this strategy multiple times.

## Suggestions for Differentiation

- Provide a variety of reading material.
- Allow some students to work with a partner.

- Use listening stations.
- Allow some students to make an oral report while others make a written report.

## Technology Adaptation

1. Create an electronic display of the information.
2. Use Teacher Tube or Animoto as a way for students to teach how to use their study guides with classmates.

## Teacher Notes

_____

_____

_____

_____

_____

_____

_____

_____

_____

## STRATEGY: PARTNER PREDICTION

### Why Use the Partner Prediction Strategy?

The purpose of the Partner Prediction Strategy (Buehl, 1997) is to provide students with an interactive strategy for sharing information from the reading with classmates.

### Types of Texts

Fiction, Non-Fiction, and Expository Text. This strategy can be easily modified for a variety of content areas.

## Grade Level Adaptability

Elementary and Secondary.

## Steps in the Process

1. Identify pre-designated places within the text for students to stop and discuss with a classmate.
2. Read the title of the selection to students and ask them to predict what they believe will be in the text.
3. Tell students they are to read to a specified stopping point and then stop to discuss the text content with a partner. Each discussion point should end with students making predictions on what they believe will be in the next section of text.
4. Continue this pattern of questioning until reading selection is finished.
5. Follow-up with teacher led discussion with the whole class.

## Engage with Bloom's Taxonomy

- *Remember:* Recall what you read from the text in as much detail as possible.
- *Understand:* Locate important vocabulary words within the text, and explain in your own words what they mean in the context of the text.
- *Apply:* How can you apply the information from the text to what has been studied in class?
- *Analyze:* What conclusions can you draw from the text?
- *Evaluate:* How could you prove or disprove information from the text?

## Benefits

- Provides structure for reading
- Encourages student discussion
- Straightforward, easy to explain and understand
- Facilitates prediction of text content
- Enjoyable for students

## Considerations

- Teacher modeling of possible questions and answers may be necessary.
- Some students may need close supervision to stay on task.

## Suggestions for Differentiation

- Provide teacher-made questions for some students.
- Use listening stations.

## Technology Adaptation

1. Use Twitter to share predictions with classmates.

## Teacher Notes

_____

_____

_____

_____

_____

_____

_____

_____

_____

## STRATEGY: PLUS, MINUS, INTERESTING (PMI)

### Why Use the PMI Strategy?

The PMI Strategy (De Bono, 1994) was designed to help students focus attention to more than one perspective and opinion. This strategy facilitates student analysis of the reading content.

## Types of Texts

Fiction, Non-Fiction, and Expository Text. This strategy can be easily modified for a variety of content areas.

## Grade Level Adaptability

Upper Elementary, Secondary, and Post-Secondary.

## Steps in the Process

1. Ask students to read or listen to a reading selection or a story.
2. Have students make three vertical columns of equal size on a sheet of paper. They should label the columns "P," "M," and "I."
3. "P" represents "Plus" or good points within the text or story.
4. "M" represents "Minus" or points of disagreement.
5. "I" represents "Interesting" information.
6. Ask students to read the text and make note of information they would include within each column.
7. Challenge students to consider a variety of perspectives.
8. When organizers are complete, ask students to share their respective lists with a partner or with a small group of students.
9. When the sharing is complete, facilitate a discussion of the material with the whole class.

## Engage with Bloom's Taxonomy

- *Remember:* List the important points within the story.
- *Understand:* Summarize the main idea from each section of text.
- *Apply:* What examples did the author use to explain the information?
- *Analyze:* How did you determine what was a "P," a "M," and an "I"?
- *Evaluate:* Compare your PMI chart to a classmate's chart. How are they the same? How are they different? Defend or modify your chart based on the comparison.

## Benefits

- Can be done individually, with a small group, or with the whole class
- Requires moderate advance preparation from the teacher
- Provides a novel method of interacting with text
- Sets a specific purpose for reading
- Helps in classroom with students having a wide range of academic ability
- Requires students to consider a variety of perspectives
- Can be easily implemented by a substitute teacher
- May serve as a guide for further study

## Considerations

- Some students may find it difficult to consider a perspective other than their own.

## Suggestions for Differentiation

- Allow some students to work in groups while others complete the assignment individually.
- Divide the columns within the class and have individuals or groups complete one column each.
- Use different scoring rubrics.

## Technology Adaptation

1. Tell students to research the topic on the Internet to find further information. Ask them to record the information on the PMI chart.
2. Ask students to create the PMI chart electronically using pictures, words, or symbols.
3. Use a classroom blog to share information from the PMI charts.

## Teacher Notes

_____

_____

_____

_____

_____

_____

_____

_____

## STRATEGY: POINT COUNTERPOINT

### Why Use the Point Counterpoint Strategy?

The purpose of the Point Counterpoint Strategy (Rogers, 1991) is to empower readers with the ability to consider a variety of interpretations of a text or reading. It encourages students to interpret the reading for themselves, as opposed to always deferring to the opinions or interpretations of teachers, texts, or others.

### Types of Texts

Fiction, Non-Fiction, and Expository Text. This strategy can be easily modified for a variety of content areas.

### Grade Level Adaptability

Secondary and Post-Secondary.

### Steps in the Process

1. Activate background knowledge by facilitating discussion related to what students already know about the topic or subject.

2. Instruct students to write ideas or responses to the reading as the text is read. This can include, but not be limited to, reflections of a personal nature, themes of the story, points of confusion, predictions of further reading, and questions for the author, teacher, or others.
3. After completion of the reading, students should discuss with others what they wrote. This can include a comparison to other ideas or a discussion of how ideas may differ, depending on interpretation.
4. Provide examples of how others may interpret the reading selection.
5. After discussion within small groups or whole class, ask students to reconsider their interpretation and decide on a final perspective.

## Engage with Bloom's Taxonomy

- *Remember:* From the reading, recall who, what, when, where, and why.
- *Understand:* Choose a question from the text and summarize.
- *Apply:* What questions would you like to ask the author?
- *Analyze:* Choose a character from the text, and write a personality profile.
- *Evaluate:* List five important pieces of information from the reading. Consider their overall importance to your understanding of the content, and place them in priority order. Be prepared to justify your answers.

## Benefits

- Provides structure for students when reading difficult and challenging material
- Provides for differentiation among students
- Facilitates a deeper understanding of the text based on their own interpretation
- Actively engages readers in the reading process
- Facilitates better preparation for reading material as an independent reader

- Encourages reflection of original ideas, as well as the ideas of others
- Facilitates critical thinking

## Considerations

- This strategy may be too difficult for readers that need a great deal of teacher support.
- If there is a lack of student background knowledge of the topic, the strategy may be unproductive.
- Some students may resist when required to "think" about their written response.

## Suggestions for Differentiation

- Provide graphic organizers of text content.
- Use leveled reading material.
- Use graphic novels.
- Provide a listening center for students to use, if they need to do so.

## Technology Adaptation

1. Ask students to research both points of view on the Internet and be prepared to share additional thoughts and perspectives.
2. Have students record their points of view and post them on Teacher Tube or Animoto. Using a scoring rubric provided by the teacher, ask students to critique video.
3. Use Google Docs to create and share student projects related to point of view.

## Teacher Notes

_____

_____

_____

_____

_____

_____

_____

_____

## STRATEGY: QUESTION, REDUCE, READ, AND DISCUSS

### Why Use the Question, Reduce, Read, and Discuss Strategy?

The purpose of the Question, Reduce, Read, and Discuss Strategy (Brunner, 2011) is to provide a comprehensive way for students and teachers to engage with text. It provides activation of background knowledge, outlining or graphic organization, and reader reflection. This strategy is particularly beneficial to students when the reading is difficult and complex.

### Types of Texts

Fiction, Non-Fiction, and Expository Text. This strategy can be easily modified for a variety of content areas.

### Grade Level Adaptability

Elementary, Secondary, and Post-Secondary.

### Steps in the Process

1. Ask students to brainstorm what they already know about the topic.
2. Provide a graphic organizer or outline of the information, and discuss the contents with the class. This can be provided on paper or with an electronic graphic organizer.
3. Set the purpose for reading by instructing students to find information on two types of information in the text. This can be

information that supports what has already been discussed and information that has not yet been discussed but is relevant.

4. Give students the reading selection, and ask them to predict the contents based on the title.
5. Tell students to read the text and be prepared to discuss new information, as well as any other material from the text that is relevant to the topic.

## Engage with Bloom's Taxonomy

- *Remember:* Make a list of the events or the author's main points.
- *Understand:* Summarize the main idea.
- *Apply:* After listing what you want to remember from the text, summarize why this information is important to know and understand.
- *Analyze:* How is what you learned from the text related to the topic?
- *Evaluate:* What is the value of learning and understand the text content? In what ways is the information relevant?

## Benefits

- Provides structure for students when reading difficult and challenging material
- Provides teacher the opportunity to pre-teach key vocabulary
- Facilitates a deeper understanding of the text
- Actively engages readers in the reading process

## Considerations

- None noted.

## Suggestions for Differentiation

- Provide graphic organizers in advance.
- Use flexible grouping.

- Pre-assess knowledge to determine the need to activate background knowledge.
- Use reading buddies.

## Technology Adaptation

1. Display the graphic organizer electronically.
2. Use Google Docs to create a graphic organizer for the class to use as a study guide.
3. Use Glogster to create a virtual poster of the lesson content.

## Teacher Notes

_____

_____

_____

_____

_____

_____

_____

_____

_____

## STRATEGY: QUESTIONING THE AUTHOR (QtA)

## Why Use the Questioning the Author Strategy?

The purpose of the QtA Strategy (Beck, McKeown, Hamilton, and Kucan, 1997) is to keep readers engaged and thinking about the information while reading a text. The questions facilitate classroom discussion for teacher and students and encourage an exchange of ideas between reader and author. This strategy is particularly beneficial to students when the reading is difficult and complex.

## Types of Texts

Fiction, Non-Fiction, and Expository Text. This strategy can be easily modified for a variety of content areas.

## Grade Level Adaptability

Upper Elementary, Secondary, and Post-Secondary.

## Steps in the Process

1. Tell students they will be reading challenging and interesting information.
2. Display the sample questions, and model how to answer the questions while reading the material. It is helpful to have students write and respond orally with answers.
3. After students understand how to use the questions and are comfortable with the process, use the questions for discussion purposes only, as opposed to requiring an answer in writing.
4. Display questions on a PowerPoint, written on a marker board, or provide as individual instructional guides. Questions should remain displayed for student reference throughout the time designated for reading.
5. Use professional judgment when deciding which questions to use with students. Some questions may need revised, eliminated, or additional questions to be added. The content of the questions will, to a large degree, be dependent on the content and purpose for reading the passage in the text.

## Engage with Bloom's Taxonomy

- *Remember:* Write or recite a timeline of events from the text.
- *Understand:* What is the main idea of the passage?
- *Apply:* What examples did the authors use to justify a specific point of view? How does the reading connect with what you already know?

- *Analyze:* What are the authors trying to help you understand?
- *Evaluate:* How did the structure of the text help you understand the content?

## Benefits

- Provides structure for students when reading difficult and challenging material
- Provides teacher flexibility with content of the questions
- Provides for differentiation among students
- Facilitates a deeper understanding of the text
- Actively engages readers in the reading process
- Helps students understand the significance of text structure
- Facilitates better preparation for reading expository material as an independent reader
- Encourages critical thinking

## Considerations

- Some students may resist when required to "think," rather than write a response.

## Suggestions for Differentiation

- Use flexible grouping.
- Use listening centers.
- Adjust questions for students based on Bloom's Taxonomy.
- Provide predetermined questions for some students.

## Technology Adaptation

1. Ask students to use electronic resources to research the author related to how he lived and other things that might be pertinent to the discussion of the book.
2. Use Google Docs to share information as students critique the work of classmates.

## Teacher Notes

_____

_____

_____

_____

_____

_____

_____

_____

## STRATEGY: READ, ENCODE, ANNOTATE, PONDER (REAP)

### Why Use the REAP Strategy?

The REAP Strategy (Eanet and Manzo, 1976) was designed to help students improve their reading comprehension of content within a text.

### Types of Texts

Fiction, Non-Fiction, and Expository Text. This strategy can be easily modified for a variety of content areas.

### Grade Level Adaptability

Elementary, Secondary, and Post-Secondary.

### Steps in the Process

1. Ask students to read the text independently.
2. Explain that the purpose for reading is to identify the main points and to restate these points in their own words.

3. Give each student note cards, and ask them to use the cards to restate what they want to remember from the text. Encourage students to write summary, thesis, critical, and question annotations.

4. Explain that there are four main types of annotations—summary annotations, thesis annotations, critical annotations, and question annotations.

5. Display an example of each type of annotation.
   - Summary—A variety of factors contributed to the beginning and the conclusion of the Civil War.
   - Thesis—The Civil War divided the country, the states, and families.
   - Critical—The Civil War resolved the issue of slavery but did not address the real issue of human rights.
   - Question—How are modern day civil wars in other countries similar and different to the American Civil War?

6. Divide the class into small groups for the purpose of sharing information from the note cards.

## Engage with Bloom's Taxonomy

- *Remember:* List the important points from the text.
- *Understand:* Create a summary annotation.
- *Apply:* What examples did the author use to explain the information?
- *Analyze:* Create a critical annotation.
- *Evaluate:* Create a question annotation.

## Benefits

- Requires little advance preparation from the teacher
- Encourages critical thinking
- Allows for consideration of more than one point of view
- Supports deeper learning and reading
- Allows interaction of note cards
- Encourages note cards to provide a study guide

## Considerations

- Initially, it may difficult for students to understand the expectations.

## Suggestions for Differentiation

- Allow students to work individually or in small groups.
- Use leveled readers.
- Limit the scope of the assignment for some students.

## Technology Adaptation

1. Tell students to research the topic on the Internet to find further information.
2. Ask students to record the information on a class blog.
3. Have students use Twitter to share information from note cards.

## Teacher Notes

_____

_____

_____

_____

_____

_____

_____

## STRATEGY: REQUEST

## Why Use the ReQuest Strategy?

The ReQuest Strategy (Manzo, 1969) was designed for the purpose of encouraging students to read and reflect on a passage by formulating questions to ask the teacher. This technique requires students to be actively involved in the reading process. It is engaging and interesting to students because it requires them to assume the role of "teacher," while the instructor assumes the role of "student."

## Types of Texts

Fiction, Non-Fiction, and Expository Text. This strategy can be easily modified for a variety of content areas.

## Grade Level Adaptability

Elementary, Secondary, and Post-Secondary.

## Steps in the Process

1. Select a reading passage and predetermine the stopping points for discussion. The stopping points should be determined by the difficulty of the material, as well as the reading abilities of the group of students. If reading comprehension is difficult for many students within the class or if the reading content is particularly challenging, the teacher should select shorter passages. If the passage is relatively simple, longer sections can be selected. It is helpful if the stopping points are where readers can make predictions related to the upcoming passage.

2. Create a list of questions for each reading selection ensuring students are required to remember, understand, apply, predict, and analyze information.

3. Tell students they will need a cover sheet to use during the lesson and have them cover all but the title of the selection.

4. Prior to reading the assignment, ask for a volunteer to read the title aloud.

5. Based on the title of the selection, ask students to predict what will be in the passage.

6. Advise students to be ready for "role reversal" as they will assume the role of teacher. The teacher will then assume the role of student. Explain the purpose for reading the selection is to formulate and answer questions.

7. After students have read the passage silently, allow them to pose questions.

8. After a number of students have had the opportunity to quiz the teacher, the roles reverse and the teacher asks questions of the students. When it is time to move to the next reading passage, pose the question, "What do you think will be in the next section we read?"

9. Students and teachers repeat this process until such time as the teacher believes the students can successfully read independently.

NOTE: It is recommended the teacher not always respond perfectly when students generate questions. Sometimes it is helpful to say, "You know, that is a good question, but I'm not completely sure of the answer. Does anyone else think he or she can answer the question correctly?" Or the teacher might say, "That is an excellent question. Is there anyone that can find the answer and volunteer to read the answer from the text to the rest of the class?"

While students should be asked to close their texts during the question/answer period, they should be allowed to skim for answers, if necessary.

### Engage with Bloom's Taxonomy

- *Remember:* Who were the main characters?
- *Understand:* Compare and contrast one character to another character. Summarize the character's response.
- *Apply:* What examples can you find that help you understand the text's contents?
- *Analyze:* What ideas justify the author's hypothesis?
- *Evaluate:* Did you agree with the author's conclusions? Why or why not?

### Benefits

- Requires active participation from the reader
- Encourages reader to consider answers to the questions posed

- Requires only moderate advance preparation from the teacher
- Can be easily implemented by a substitute teacher
- Encourages positive student attitudes toward strategy
- Encourages teacher modeling of higher-level questioning and responses
- Encourages silent reading
- Helpful in classroom where students have a wide range of academic ability
- Encourages teachers to "think aloud" with students relating to how answers were formulated
- Works one on one, with small groups, and with whole classes of students
- Breaks the passage into manageable parts for students and teacher

## Considerations

- The strategy may slow the reading rate of the advanced readers.
- Students may need support to ask complex and higher order questions.

## Suggestions for Differentiation

- Use leveled text.
- Use graphic novels.
- Require students to design questions at specific levels of Bloom's Taxonomy.
- Allow students to work with a partner.

## Technology Adaptation

1. None noted.

## Teacher Notes

_____

_____

_____

_____

_____

_____

## STRATEGY: SELECTIVE READING GUIDE

### Why Use the Selective Reading Guide Strategy?

The purpose of the Selective Reading Guide Strategy (Cunningham and Shablak, 1975) is to help students understand major ideas and supporting details with a text. This strategy will also teach students how to read with flexibility.

### Types of Texts

Fiction, Non-Fiction, and Expository Text. This strategy can be easily modified for a variety of content areas.

### Grade Level Adaptability

Elementary and Secondary.

### Steps in the Process

1. Identify the major concepts within the text.
2. Mark within the teacher text the main ideas as well as the important details.
3. Ask students to open their texts. After activating background knowledge, ask students to read to a designated point.
4. After students finish reading, ask them to follow as the teacher thinks aloud. Particular attention should be paid to main idea and supporting details.

5. Discuss with students how main idea and supporting details were identified.
6. Ask students to take notes during class discussion.
7. Repeat the process until text selection is completed.

## Engage with Bloom's Taxonomy

- *Remember:* What do you remember about what was read?
- *Understand:* What is the main idea of the passage?
- *Apply:* How does the information from the text relate to other information learned in this unit of instruction?
- *Analyze:* What are the authors trying to help you understand?
- *Evaluate:* How did the structure of the text help you identify the main idea and supporting details?

## Benefits

- Provides structure for reading
- Activates background knowledge
- Supports teacher modeling
- Straightforward and easy to explain and understand
- Provides a helpful tool for students to use when reading independently
- Can be done with small or large groups
- Supports independent reading

## Considerations

- This strategy may be too time consuming.

## Suggestions for Differentiation

- Use leveled text.
- Allow students to work individually or within flexible groups.

## Technology Adaptation

1. Ask students to take notes, display the notes electronically, and share with the class.

## Teacher Notes

_____

_____

_____

_____

_____

_____

_____

_____

## STRATEGY: SILENT WITH SUPPORT

### Why Use the Silent with Support Strategy?

The purpose of the Silent with Support Strategy (Lamme and Beckett, 1992) is to assist students with reading comprehension when reading silently.

### Types of Texts

Fiction, Non-Fiction, and Expository Text. This strategy can be easily modified for a variety of content areas.

### Grade Level Adaptability

Elementary and Secondary.

### Steps in the Process

1. Place students in pairs or in small groups.
2. Ask them to read the selection silently while sitting with a partner.
3. Explain that they may consult with their group if they have questions or need assistance during the reading.

## Engage with Bloom's Taxonomy

- *Remember:* What do you remember about the reading selection?
- *Understand:* What is the main idea of the passage?
- *Apply:* What information from the text would best demonstrate that you understand the content?
- *Analyze:* What inferences can you make from what you read?
- *Evaluate:* What is the most interesting information from the text? What influenced your choice?

## Benefits

- Provides purposeful discussion among students
- Emphasizes the importance of comprehension during silent reading

## Considerations

- If most students seem confused from the text, the strategy will lose its effectiveness.

## Suggestions for Differentiation

- Use flexible grouping.
- Use listening centers.
- Provide a graphic organizer with the text content to selected students.

## Technology Adaptation

1. Use a class blog to record important information from the text.
2. Create an electronic visual display of the information.

## Teacher Notes

_____

_____

---
---
---
---
---
---
---

## STRATEGY: SPECIAL POWERS, PROBLEM SOLVING, ALTERNATIVE VIEWPOINTS, WHAT IF, NEXT (SPAWN)

### Why Use the SPAWN Strategy?

The purpose of the SPAWN Strategy (Martin, Martin, and O'Brien, 1984) is to encourage students to examine complex issues while thinking critically about the reading selection.

### Types of Texts

Fiction, Non-Fiction, and Expository Text. This strategy can be easily modified for a variety of content areas.

### Grade Level Adaptability

Upper Elementary, Secondary, and Post-Secondary.

### Steps in the Process

1. Assign the reading selection.
2. Ask students to expand their thinking about the text by considering the following:
   - Special powers—If you had special powers, how could you impact the event described in the reading?
   - Problem solving—How might you solve the problem differently than what was described in the text?

- Alternative viewpoints—If you were a participant in the story, how might you explain your point of view?
- What if—What if events and facts were different? How would that impact the information?
- Next—What would you do next?

3. After students have written responses to the prompts, ask them to share with classmates.

## Engage with Bloom's Taxonomy

- *Remember:* Recall what you read from the text in as much detail as possible.
- *Understand:* Summarize what you read.
- *Apply:* How is this information useful to your understanding of the subject?
- *Analyze:* How are your suggestions different from the author's information?
- *Evaluate:* Why do you believe your ideas might be better than a classmate's ideas? Do you believe your ideas were better than what the character did within the text?

## Benefits

- Encourages student discussion
- Provides a novel way to encourage critical thinking
- Encourages students to think beyond the obvious

## Considerations

- Teacher modeling of possible questions and answers may be necessary.
- Some students may need close supervision to stay on task.
- The strategy may be confusing to explain and understand.
- Students may resist the activity initially.
- The strategy may be too time consuming.

## Suggestions for Differentiation

- Provide graphic organizers for some students.
- Allow some students to respond in writing while others respond verbally.
- Provide additional guided practice for some students.

## Technology Adaptation

1. Use Animoto to create videos of students role-playing their ideas.

## Teacher Notes

_____

_____

_____

_____

_____

_____

_____

_____

_____


## STRATEGY: THAT WAS THEN, THIS IS NOW

## Why Use the That Was Then, This Is Now Strategy?

The That Was Then, This Is Now Strategy (McLaughlin and Allen, 2002) was designed to encourage students to think about what they already know and to relate the information to what they read from a text.

## Types of Texts

Fiction, Non-Fiction, and Expository Text. This strategy can be easily modified for a variety of content areas.

## Grade Level Adaptability

Elementary, Secondary, and Post-Secondary.

## Steps in the Process

1. Identify a topic and introduce it to students.
2. Divide students into groups of 3–4.
3. Ask students to draw a vertical line in the center of a sheet of paper.
4. At the top of the column on the left, ask students to write the words "That was then . . ."
5. At the top of the column on the right, ask students to write the words "This is now . . ."
6. In the column on the left, ask students to use illustrations to represent some of the things they already know about the topic.
7. At the bottom of the left side of the paper tell students to write a summary statement. This statement can be tied to the drawing, or it can provide supplemental information.
8. Ask students to read the text.
9. After completing the reading assignment, instruct students to draw a representation of what they learned from the reading in the column on the right.
10. Tell them to write a summary statement under the column on the right.
11. Ask students to compare and contrast the before and after sketches with a partner, with other groups, or with the whole class.

## Engage with Bloom's Taxonomy

- *Remember:* Ask students to draw pictures based on the factual context of the text.

- *Understand:* Using symbols, draw the new information to what you know.
- *Analyze:* Using non-linguistic representations, prioritize the information from the text.
- *Evaluate:* Using a scoring rubric, evaluate the work of classmates.

## Benefits

- Can be done individually or with a small group
- Encourages creativity
- Requires only moderate advance preparation from the teacher
- Provides a novel method of activating background knowledge
- Facilitates mental imaging
- Helps in classroom where students have a wide range of academic ability
- Requires students to compare and contrast information

## Considerations

- Some students may resist due to a perceived lack of skill related to drawing and sketching.
- Students may need some background knowledge of the topic prior to beginning the assignment.

## Suggestions for Differentiation

- Allow some students to work individually while others work in groups.
- Allow some students to use a combination of words and symbols.
- Provide possible non-linguistic representation. Ask students to add some of their own.

## Technology Adaptation

1. Have students use electronic images to design the visual product.
2. Use Twitter to provide feedback.

## Teacher Notes

_____

_____

_____

_____

_____

_____

_____

_____

## STRATEGY: THINK, PAIR, SHARE

### Why Use the Think, Pair, Share Strategy?

The Think, Pair, Share Strategy (Bromley and Modlo, 1997) was developed to support students as they read challenging text.

### Types of Texts

Fiction, Non-Fiction, and Expository Text. This strategy can be easily modified for a variety of content areas.

### Grade Level Adaptability

Elementary and Secondary.

### Steps in the Process

1. Pose a question to the class related to the reading.
2. After students have considered the question, ask them to share responses with a partner.
3. Pose another question, and ask students to read to find the answer.
4. Have students share their answers with a partner.

## Engage with Bloom's Taxonomy

- *Remember:* What are three important details from the reading selection?
- *Understand:* Summarize what you read to your partner.
- *Apply:* How can you use the information from the text?
- *Analyze:* How could you categorize or classify information from the reading selection?
- *Evaluate:* How could you prioritize the information from the text? What is most important? What is least important?

## Benefits

- Requires little advance preparation from the teacher
- Provides for organized discussion of reading material
- Sets a specific purpose for reading
- Can be easily implemented by a substitute teacher
- Makes a good activity to support reviewing for assessment

## Considerations

- Some students may need additional guidance and monitoring

## Suggestions for Differentiation

- Allow for flexible grouping of students.
- Adjust amount of information for activation of background knowledge.
- Use teacher or student directed questions.

## Technology Adaptation

1. Allow students to use an electronic device to communicate with partner

## Teacher Notes

_____

_____

_____

_____

_____

_____

_____

_____

_____

## STRATEGY: WE'RE ALL IN THIS TOGETHER

### Why Use the We're All in This Together Strategy?

The purpose of the We're All in This Together Strategy is to provide students the opportunity to research and become the class "expert" on a specified topic or topics.

### Types of Texts

Fiction, Non-Fiction, and Expository Text. This strategy can be easily modified for a variety of content areas.

### Grade Level Adaptability

Upper Elementary, Secondary, and Post-Secondary.

### Steps in the Process

1. Divide the text into manageable parts.
2. Assign an individual or groups of individuals to read the text for the purpose of explaining the content to classmates during a whole class discussion.
3. Ask each group or individual to be prepared to teach the content with the assistance of a graphic organizer they have designed.

4. At designated times throughout the lesson, ask for the "experts" on a given subject or topic to explain the content to the class. NOTE: This can be an informal or formal presentation.

## Engage with Bloom's Taxonomy

- *Remember:* What do you remember from the text?
- *Understand:* Summarize the author's thoughts.
- *Apply:* Prepare a graphic organizer that explains the most important concepts from the reading.
- *Analyze:* What information from the text is important to the overall understanding of the content?
- *Evaluate:* Using a predesigned rubric, evaluate the student presentations and graphic organizer.

## Benefits

- Provides a framework for students when reading difficult and challenging material
- Provides teacher flexibility and the opportunity to differentiate instruction depending on the content of the reading selections provided to individual students
- Facilitates a deeper understanding of the text
- Actively engages students in the process of reading for a purpose
- Facilitates retention by teaching information to other students
- Can be easily implemented by a substitute teacher

## Considerations

- Students with little background knowledge of the topic may struggle with this activity.
- This activity may be too time consuming.

## Suggestions for Differentiation

- Group students based on topic interest.
- Limit the scope of the assignment for some students.

- Provide varying levels of activating background knowledge.
- Use leveled text.
- Allow students to choose between the type of presentation to be made, e.g., panel discussion, individual presentation, electronic resources.

## Technology Adaptation

1. Ask students to use Internet resources to support the text.
2. Post student information on a class blog to be used as a study guide.
3. Ask students to provide individual feedback to classmates through the use of Twitter.

## Teacher Notes

_____

_____

_____

_____

_____

_____

_____

_____

# STUDY SKILLS

Helping students develop study habits that are effective, efficient, and research based has been a concern of educators for many years. Some teachers have made the assumption that, because students were taught study skills strategies in earlier grades, they would then use those strategies when working independently. Unfortunately, that has not always been the case.

As educators know and understand, teaching is not telling. Until such time as students use and embrace these study skills strategies on a routine and regular basis, classroom teachers must continue to use direct instruction as a means of reinforcing and encouraging everyone to study in the most efficient manner possible. For most students, it is not a matter of studying harder; it is all about studying smarter.

Most individuals experience difficulty with concentration from time to time, and students must develop the ability to cope with both internal and external distractions. While brain compatible teaching strategies should be used routinely in all schools, teachers should also include activities that facilitate the development of student self-discipline. This will be necessary if students are going to be successful in school and prepared for life during the twenty-first century.

According to Walter Pauk, noted study skills expert, what students want and need are practical methods that work. They want to

CHAPTER 3

get the task done, and they want it done with the least amount of
time and effort. And who can really blame them?

This chapter is designed to provide teachers with strategies students can easily use to become self-sufficient, independent, and
successful life-long learners. Because all of these strategies support
reading comprehension, they could have been included in chapter 2. However, because they also encourage student independence
and self-directed learning, they were included in this chapter of
study skills strategies.

The activities include teaching the structure and features within
a text, note taking, using legitimate resources, skimming, monitoring reading comprehension, and self-assessment. Each strategy was
selected based on its ease of use, effectiveness, and student-friendly
steps in the process.

Used within the context of a specific content area, these instructional methods will facilitate student learning; however, teachers
should routinely reinforce the idea that students should use the
strategies to support their own learning, even when the teacher is not
there to remind them to do so. Particular emphasis should be given
to the idea that these are not just activities to be completed as part of
a homework assignment; rather, they are ways to learn information
both inside *and* outside of the school setting. When students begin to
routinely use these strategies on their own, it will make reading and
understanding the written word easier. It's as simple as that.


## STRATEGY: BOOK TOUR

### Why Use Book Tour Strategy?

The purpose of the Book Tour Strategy (Buehl, 2001) is to understand how to use the features of a text to support understanding.

### Types of Texts

Non-Fiction and Expository Text. This strategy can be easily modified for a variety of content areas.

## Grade Level Adaptability

Elementary and Secondary.

## Steps in the Process

1. Explain to students they will be on a book tour to help them use the text to study more efficiently.
2. Have them open their books and direct them to the following features:
   - Table of contents
   - Titles
   - Subtitles
   - Graphs, charts, and pictures
   - Margin notes
   - Bold and italicized words
   - Outlines
   - Questions
   - Index
   - Glossary
   - References
3. At the completion of the book tour, ask students to use a different text to design a book tour for classmates.
4. Have students demonstrate a book tour to classmates.

## Engage with Bloom's Taxonomy

- *Remember:* What are the features of a book that help you understand the content?
- *Understand:* Using your own words, define three text features.
- *Apply:* Design a book tour for an online source.
- *Analyze:* Give an example of how a specific text feature supports understanding.
- *Evaluate:* Which text features were the most helpful? List them in the order of importance, and be prepared to explain the reason for the choice of priorities.

## Benefits

- Activates background knowledge
- Supports independent learning across the content fields
- Requires little advance preparation from the teacher
- Works one on one, with small groups, and with the whole class
- Encourages peer-to-peer discussion

## Considerations

- This activity is best suited for the first few weeks of a semester.

## Suggestions for Differentiation

- Allow student to choose individual books for the book tour
- Recommend students work in small groups designing the tour, depending upon genre of the chosen text

## Technology Adaptation

1. Ask students to examine the text features of online resources, websites, etc.

## Teacher Notes

_____

_____

_____

_____

_____

_____

_____

## STRATEGY: CLUSTERING

### Why Use the Clustering Strategy?

The purpose of the Clustering Strategy (Vacca and Vacca, 2008) is to help students approach pre-writing in an organized and systematic manner. It will help to connect ideas and categories of information.

### Types of Texts

Fiction, Non-Fiction, and Expository Text. This strategy can be easily modified for a variety of content areas.

### Grade Level Adaptability

Elementary, Secondary, and Post-Secondary.

### Steps in the Process

1. Provide students with a word and direct them to write the word in the middle of a sheet of paper.
2. Ask students to draw a circle around the word.
3. As they think about the word, ask students to write related words around the original word, using lines to connect the words in an organizational manner.
4. When a different thought is considered, ask students to draw connecting lines between the words that are connected and the original nucleus word. The Word Cluster will be similar in appearance to a Word Web.
5. Ask students to review the cluster, and place the thoughts in some type of order that makes sense, noting which pieces of information should be in an introduction, main paragraph, or concluding paragraph.
6. Students should use this graphic organizer as a pre-writing exercise. After the Word Cluster is completed, direct students to use these thoughts as an outline for formal writing.

## Engage with Bloom's Taxonomy

- *Remember:* Explain how and when to use the Clustering Strategy.
- *Understand:* How does using the Clustering Strategy support learning?
- *Apply:* Use a topic from the text, and design a pre-writing cluster.
- *Analyze:* Compare and contrast one of your papers where you used the Clustering Strategy to a sample of your writing when you did not use the strategy.
- *Evaluate:* Review the work of other classmates. Did their use of the Clustering Strategy help make the writing product better? In what ways was it better? How could they have improved their word cluster?

## Benefits

- Provides a framework for pre-writing
- Provides teacher flexibility and the opportunity to differentiate instruction depending on the nucleus words given to each group
- Supports study skills independence and is easily understood by students
- Actively engages students in the process of pre-writing
- Easily applies to all content areas
- Can be a pre-reading or post-reading activity

## Considerations

- Students should be familiar with words before using this strategy.

## Suggestions for Differentiation

- Provide words of varying complexity.
- Group students based on word complexity.
- Based on student choice, allow for product variation.

## Technology Adaptation

1. Ask students to display their word clusters electronically.
2. Ask students to critique the word clusters of classmates and give feedback through Twitter.

## Teacher Notes

_____

_____

_____

_____

_____

_____

_____

_____

## STRATEGY: CORNELL NOTE TAKING

### Why Use Cornell Note Taking Strategy?

The primary purpose of the Cornell Note Taking Strategy (Pauk, 1974) is to provide students an organized and efficient method of taking lecture notes or notes from a text. This note taking system provides an easy-to-use study guide.

### Types of Texts

Non-Fiction and Expository Text. This strategy can be easily modified for a variety of content areas.

### Grade Level Adaptability

Upper Elementary, Secondary, and Post-Secondary.

### Steps in the Process

1. Tell students to draw a line vertically on the left side of a piece of paper.
2. Instruct them to write important information from the lecture or text in the column on the right side of the paper.

3. After notes are completed, tell students to review the notes and write questions from the content in the margin on the left side of the paper.
4. Ask students to cover the right column, exposing only the questions on the left. Students should self quiz or work within a small group of students to learn the important concepts.

### Engage with Bloom's Taxonomy

- *Remember:* How do you prepare paper for taking notes using the Cornell Note Taking Method?
- *Understand:* Explain to a classmate the benefits of taking notes in that manner.
- *Apply:* Using the textbook, take notes over a chapter's content using this method.
- *Analyze:* Compare and contrast this note taking method with a different type of note taking method.
- *Evaluate:* Think about this note taking method related to assessment, understanding content, ease of use, and efficiency. When is it the best approach to note taking? When might it not be useful?

### Benefits

- Promotes active listening
- Provides a systematic method for note taking
- Provides a ready-made study guide for review
- Can be easily implemented
- Supports retention of material

### Considerations

- Some students may resist if they have already developed their own method for taking notes.

### Suggestions for Differentiation

- Allow some students to work with a partner and photocopy notes.

- Encourage the use of pictures and symbols, as well as words.
- Provide students with a partially completed note taking guide. Ask them to fill in the missing word or words.
- Transfer notes to note cards for studying.

## Technology Adaptation

1. Ask students to record notes electronically and share them through a class blog.
2. Display an electronic display of a student's notes that were well prepared. This can be used as a prototype for other students.

## Teacher Notes

_____

_____

_____

_____

_____

_____

_____

_____

_____

## STRATEGY: EXPECTATION OUTLINE

## Why Use the Expectation Outline Strategy?

The purpose of the Expectation Outline Strategy (Spiegel, 1981) is to help students activate background knowledge by asking questions about the text. Originally designed for non-fiction, it can be easily adapted for a narrative reading selection.

## Types of Texts

Fiction, Non-Fiction, and Expository Text. This strategy can be easily modified for a variety of content areas.

## Grade Level Adaptability

Elementary, Secondary, and Post-Secondary.

## Steps in the Process

1. Ask students to preview and skim what they will be reading.
2. Pose the question, "What do you think you are going to read?"
3. Ask students to respond in the form of a question.
4. Record the student questions and inquire as to why they believe the question is relevant.
5. Ask students to group the questions in a manner that makes sense to them.
6. After questions are grouped, ask students to label question groupings.
7. Add questions that will encourage students to read for deeper meaning.
8. Direct students to read the text selection for the purpose of answering the proposed questions.
9. Debrief the exercise with students by explaining how they can use this activity as an independent reader or when working with a group of classmates in a study group.

## Engage with Bloom's Taxonomy

- *Remember:* Explain how and when to use the Expectation Outline Strategy.
- *Understand:* How does using the Expectation Outline Strategy support their understanding of the content material?
- *Apply:* Design an Expectation Outline without teacher assistance.
- *Analyze:* How is this textbook strategy different from what you have done in the past? Do the differences make it more helpful or less helpful?

- *Evaluate:* Can you think of a more thorough way of introducing text material to a reader? Did the strategy support your understanding of the content? Be specific.

## Benefits

- Provides a framework for activating background knowledge
- Provides teacher flexibility and the opportunity to differentiate instruction depending on the questions generated
- Supports study skills independence and is easily understood by students
- Supports student engagement
- Easily applies to all content areas

## Considerations

- If students lack initial background knowledge, it will be challenging to generate meaningful questions.

## Suggestions for Differentiation

- Use leveled texts.
- Use flexible grouping.
- Allow the most challenged readers to hear the text content at a listening center.
- Rather than previewing the printed text, allow students to preview a graphic organizer that represents the text content.
- Ask students to use non-linguistic representations for answers to the questions.

## Technology Adaptation

1. Ask students to display their questions and answers electronically.
2. Use a class blog to display questions and answers.
3. Use Google Docs to support student collaboration of ideas.

## Teacher Notes

---
---
---
---
---
---
---
---
---

## STRATEGY: GRAPHIC INFORMATION

### Why Use Graphic Information Strategy?

The purpose of the Graphic Information Strategy is to help students understand how to efficiently interpret pictures, graphs, and diagrams.

### Types of Texts

Fiction, Non-Fiction, and Expository Text. This strategy can be easily modified for a variety of content areas.

### Grade Level Adaptability

Elementary, Secondary, and Post-Secondary.

### Steps in the Process

1. Explain to students that pictures, graphic organizers, and diagrams help to explain complicated text.
2. Find a graphic or picture in the text, and ask students to "read" it.

3. Instruct them to survey the graphic or picture by reading the title.
4. Instruct students to pay close attention to detail, headings, etc.
5. Ask students to skim the text to help understand the connection between the text and the picture or graphic.
6. Direct students to write a brief paragraph summarizing what the picture or graphic is helping them to understand.
7. Ask students to get into small groups to share their interpretations.

## Engage with Bloom's Taxonomy

- *Remember:* What is the purpose for using the Graphic Information Strategy?
- *Understand:* Explain to a classmate why this strategy helps to support understanding of text.
- *Apply:* View a different graphic, and explain to a partner how to "read" it.
- *Analyze:* Why are some graphics more helpful than others?
- *Evaluate:* Compare pictures within a text to another type of graphic organizer. Which one is most helpful in understanding the content? Explain why each visual representation is helpful or not so helpful.
- *Create:* Choose a graphic that is confusing to the reader. Redesign it so that it is more helpful to the reader.

## Benefits

- Activates background knowledge
- Supports independent learning across the content fields
- Requires little advance preparation from the teacher
- Works one on one, with small groups, and with the whole class
- Encourages peer-to-peer discussion

## Considerations

- Authors and publishers make decisions related to which and what types of graphic organizers to include in a text. This decision may not be based on the background knowledge of some readers.

- Some graphic organizers are more confusing than the actual text. Explain to students that the organizer and text should be "read" as one unit.

## Technology Adaptation

1. Ask students to examine the graphic organizers and pictures of online resources, websites, etc.
2. Use Edmodo or Twitter to share information among students.

## Teacher Notes

_____

_____

_____

_____

_____

_____

_____

_____

## STRATEGY: GUIDED READING AND SUMMARIZING (GRASP)

### Why Use the GRASP Strategy?

The purpose of the GRASP Strategy (Hayes, 1989) is to teach students how to independently summarize what they read.

### Types of Texts

Fiction, Non-Fiction, and Expository Text. This strategy can be easily modified for a variety of content areas.

## Grade Level Adaptability

Upper Elementary, Secondary, and Post-Secondary.

## Steps in the Process

1. Assign a passage for reading.
2. Tell students to read the passage silently for the purpose of remembering all they can related to content and then brainstorm and record all they can remember.
3. Discuss what students remember.
4. Instruct students to reread the passage for the purpose of adding to their list.
5. Have students organize their lists and put information into categories.
6. Ask students to use the written information to write a summary of the material.
7. Emphasize to students this is a strategy they should use routinely when studying.

## Engage with Bloom's Taxonomy

- *Remember:* Write down as many things as you can remember from the reading.
- *Understand:* Make an outline of the information from the brainstormed listing.
- *Apply:* How is the information listed important to the overall instructional objectives?
- *Analyze:* Compare and contrast your list with a classmate's listing.
- *Evaluate:* After reviewing the lists of classmates, which lists were most accurate and complete? On what did you make your determination?

## Benefits

- Provides opportunity for individual work or a collaborative effort

- Encourages attention to detail and student engagement
- Takes little teacher preparation
- Straightforward and easy to explain and understand
- Helps students understand how to write a summary in a systematic manner
- Provides a purpose for reading
- Can be easily implemented by a substitute teacher
- May be used as an ongoing activity while the book is being read

## Considerations

- This strategy may be too time consuming for some students and some topics.

## Suggestions for Differentiation

- Allow some students to work individually and others to work with a small group.
- Have selected students develop a scoring rubric for the assignment.
- Allow some students to produce an electronic document while others complete the assignment using paper and pencil.
- Use leveled text.
- Provide listening centers for some students to use.

## Technology Adaptation

1. Use Twitter or Edmodo to give feedback.
2. Use Google Docs to share and edit summaries.

## Teacher Notes

_____

_____

_____

_____

_____

_____

_____

_____

_____

## STRATEGY: NOTE TAKING FOR LEARNING

### Why Use Note Taking for Learning Strategy?

The primary purpose of the Note Taking for Learning Strategy (Palmatier, 1971) is to provide students an organized and efficient method of organizing class notes or notes from a text. This note taking system provides an easy-to-use study guide. This strategy provides a means for reviewing notes.

### Types of Texts

Non-Fiction and Expository Text. This strategy can be easily modified for a variety of content areas.

### Grade Level Adaptability

Secondary and Post-Secondary.

### Steps in the Process

1.  Tell students to record notes on the right side of the margin of notebook paper.
2.  Immediately following the lecture, ask students to organize notes while the ideas and concepts are fresh in their memories.
3.  When organizing the notes, tell students to place labels related to the content in the left side margin of the paper.
4.  Tell students to collaborate with a partner and add to their notes.

5. Explain to students that, when studying from these notes, they should only display the left side margin to self-quiz the information from the right side of the margin.

## Engage with Bloom's Taxonomy

- *Remember:* How do you prepare paper for taking notes using the Note Taking for Learning Method?
- *Understand:* Explain to a classmate the benefits of taking notes in this manner.
- *Apply:* Using the textbook, take notes over a chapter's content using this method.
- *Analyze:* Compare and contrast this note taking method with a different type of note taking method.
- *Evaluate:* Think about this note taking method related to assessment, understanding content, ease of use, and efficiency. When is it the best approach to note taking? When might it not be useful?

## Benefits

- Promotes active listening
- Provides a systematic method for note taking
- Provides a ready-made study guide for review
- Can be easily implemented
- Supports retention of material

## Considerations

- Some students may resist if they have already developed their own method for taking notes.

## Suggestions for Differentiation

- Allow some students to work with a partner.
- Encourage the use of pictures and symbols, as well as words.
- Provide students with a partially completed note taking guide. Ask them to fill in the missing word or words.

## Technology Adaptation

1. Ask students to record notes electronically and share them through a class blog.
2. Display a model of this note taking strategy on a class website.

## Teacher Notes

_____

_____

_____

_____

_____

_____

_____

_____

## STRATEGY: PARAPHRASING

## Why Use the Paraphrasing Strategy?

The purpose of the Paraphrasing Strategy (Schumaker, Denton, and Deshler, 1984) is to teach students how to summarize information from non-fiction texts.

## Types of Texts

Non-Fiction and Expository Text. This strategy can be easily modified for a variety of content areas.

## Grade Level Adaptability

Upper Elementary, Secondary, and Post-Secondary.

## Steps in the Process

1. Define paraphrasing to students and ask them to paraphrase the content from the text as it is read. Explain that they should READ a paragraph, ASK themselves to state the main idea and details, and then PUT this information into their own words (RAP).
2. In looking for the main idea, tell students to ask, "What is the paragraph about? What does it say?"
3. Tell students to locate details that help explain the main idea.
4. Ask students to paraphrase each paragraph of the assigned text. Explain that their paraphrase should include complete thoughts, be accurate, make sense, and use the student's own words.
5. Explain to students that by thinking and talking to themselves using RAP they will more easily understand and remember what is read.

## Engage with Bloom's Taxonomy

- *Remember:* What do you remember from the text?
- *Understand:* Using your own words, tell a classmate the contents of the paragraph.
- *Apply:* How is the information from the text important to the overall instructional objectives?
- *Analyze:* What conclusions can you draw from what you have read?
- *Evaluate:* How could you prioritize the paraphrased information?

## Benefits

- Provides opportunity for individual work or a collaborative effort
- Encourages attention to detail and student engagement
- Takes little teacher preparation
- Straightforward and easy to explain and understand

- Helps students understand how to summarize in a systematic manner
- Provides a purpose for reading
- Can be easily implemented by a substitute teacher
- May be used as an ongoing activity while the book is being read

## Considerations

- This strategy may be too time consuming for some students.

## Suggestions for Differentiation

- Allow some students to work individually and others to work with a small group.
- Share paraphrased information through a class blog.
- Provide a listening center that includes the content.
- Provide graphic organizers of the text content.

## Technology Adaptation

1. Use Twitter or Edmodo to give feedback.
2. Use Google Docs to share and edit summaries.

## Teacher Notes

_____

_____

_____

_____

_____

_____

_____

_____

## STRATEGY: PREPLAN, LIST, ACTIVATE, AND EVALUATE (PLAE)

### Why Use the PLAE Strategy?

The purpose of the PLAE Strategy (Nist and Simpson, 1984) is to provide students with a system for studying that helps to monitor their learning.

### Types of Texts

Fiction, Non-Fiction, and Expository Text. This strategy can be easily modified for a variety of content areas.

### Grade Level Adaptability

Upper Elementary, Secondary, and Post-Secondary.

### Steps in the Process

1. Tell students they will learn a study strategy for all content areas.
2. Display the letters P L A E and explain the acronym.
3. Ask students to identify a goal for the study session. Suggested goals might include learning vocabulary, creating note cards, understanding the main idea, studying for a test, etc.
4. Ask students to list study methods that might work toward accomplishing the study goal.
5. Have students discuss with classmates which strategies would be most efficient and effective.
6. Have students choose the type of study plan that would work best.
7. Ask students to use the preferred method of study while monitoring its effectiveness.
8. After using the study method for a sufficient amount of time, tell students to evaluate how effective the method was in learning the content.

## Engage with Bloom's Taxonomy

- *Remember:* Explain the PLAE Strategy.
- *Understand:* What makes the PLAE Strategy an effective method for learning information?
- *Apply:* Explain to a classmate how to use the PLAE Strategy in another content area.
- *Analyze:* Explain why one strategy would work better than another.
- *Evaluate:* In what ways could you evaluate different study methods?

## Benefits

- Encourages metacognition and self-reflection
- Provides teacher flexibility and the opportunity to differentiate instruction depending on questions generated
- Supports study skills independence
- Easily applied to all content areas

## Considerations

- If students have been previously unsuccessful with study skills, they may lack sufficient information to make comparisons.

## Suggestions for Differentiation

- Provide a variety of study skills strategies from which students could choose.
- Use flexible grouping.

## Technology Adaptation

1. Ask students to justify choice of study strategy using Twitter or Edmodo.
2. Use a class blog to discuss and evaluate student selected studying methods.

3.  Have students use Teacher Tube or Animoto to explain the preferred note taking strategy to classmates.

## Teacher Notes

_____

_____

_____

_____

_____

_____

_____

## STRATEGY: PREDICT, ORGANIZE, REHEARSE, PRACTICE, EVALUATE (PORPE)

### Why Use the PORPE Strategy?

The PORPE Strategy (Simpson, 1986) was designed to help students when required to take essay examinations.

### Types of Texts

Fiction, Non-Fiction, and Expository Text. This strategy can be easily modified for a variety of content areas.

### Grade Level Adaptability

Upper Elementary, Secondary, and Post-Secondary.

### Steps in the Process

1.  After studying unit content, ask students to use Bloom's Taxonomy to predict and formulate possible essay questions.

2. Ask students to share their possible questions with classmates.
3. Tell students to organize possible answers to the essay questions by brainstorming individually or with a friend.
4. Instruct students to rehearse the possible answers until such time as it goes into their memory.
5. Have students practice recalling the answers to the possible essay questions.
6. Tell students to self-evaluate the quality of their essay answers.

## Engage with Bloom's Taxonomy

- *Remember*: What does the acronym PORPE mean?
- *Understand:* Using your owns words, explain the PORPE Procedure to a classmate.
- *Apply:* Explain how this study method could be used in other content areas.
- *Analyze*: Think of the steps in the process of the PORPE Strategy. Why does this strategy work? Why might it not work?
- *Evaluate*: Evaluate the usefulness of this type of study method in math, social studies, science, and English.

## Benefits

- Can be done individually, with a small group, or with the whole class
- Requires moderate advance preparation from the teacher
- Provides a novel method of studying content
- Easily adapted for independent studying
- Serves as a study guide for students that lack a successful method of study
- Helps students monitor comprehension

## Considerations

- This strategy may be too time consuming for some students.

## Suggestions for Differentiation

- Share student responses on a class blog.
- Use flexible time amounts for guided practice.
- Allow students to share information among groups and with individuals.
- Provide graphic organizers.
- Allow students to work with partners.

## Technology Adaptation

1. Use Glogster to create a media presentation of the information.
2. Have students post to Teacher Tube to critique a variety of study skills methods.

## Teacher Notes

_____

_____

_____

_____

_____

_____

_____

_____

## STRATEGY: RATE YOURSELF

## Why Use the Rate Yourself Strategy?

The purpose of the Rate Yourself Strategy is to help students understand how to increase and improve their reading rate.

## Types of Texts

Fiction, Non-Fiction, and Expository Text. This strategy can be easily modified for a variety of content areas.

## Grade Level Adaptability

Upper Elementary, Secondary, and Post-Secondary.

## Steps in the Process

1. Explain to students that reading rate is measured by words per minute. However, help them understand they are not reading if it does not include comprehension of what is read. Being able to remember and understand what is read is the most important aspect of reading.
2. Tell students they should read different subjects at different rates, depending on the difficulty of the text and that improving the rate of reading takes repeated practice and concerted effort.
3. Discuss the reading behaviors that slow the rate—moving lips, vocalizing, reading one word at a time, and reading everything at the same reading rate.
4. Teach skimming skills—read title, introduction, headings, italicized or bold print, diagrams, maps, and pictures.
5. Ask students to review the format of the text and use the format to determine the most important information.
6. Remind students to read the first paragraph, the last paragraph, and then what is in the middle.
7. Provide something relatively easy for students to read. Remind them that increasing the rate of reading takes practice.
8. Direct students to a more complicated text, and ask them to consciously use the suggested strategies.
9. Remind students they should spend time reading things that are easy for them to read. Engaging with text during discretionary time can increase reading rate.

## Engage with Bloom's Taxonomy

- *Remember:* What is a reading rate?
- *Understand:* What are some things that interfere with reading speed? How do they interfere?
- *Apply:* Why is it important to improve a reading rate?
- *Analyze:* Think of how you read. What behaviors reduce your personal reading rate?
- *Evaluate:* After practicing some of the suggested ways to increase speed of reading, which ones were most effective to you as a reader?

## Benefits

- Supports student metacognitive awareness
- Takes little teacher preparation
- Straightforward and easy to explain and understand
- May be used as an ongoing activity while book is being read

## Considerations

- Not all students need help with adjusting reading rate.

## Suggestions for Differentiation

- Use leveled text.
- Allow more practice time for some students.

## Technology Adaptation

1. Use Twitter or Edmodo for students to describe their experience with the strategy.
2. Ask students to use the reading strategy with a passage from an electronic source.

## Teacher Notes

_____

_____

_____

_____

_____

_____

_____

_____

_____

## STRATEGY: RESOURCE COURSE

### Why Use the Resource Course Strategy?

The purpose of the Resource Course Strategy (Ellery and Rosembom, 2011) is to help students understand how to use a glossary or thesaurus to analyze vocabulary associated with a specific content area.

### Types of Texts

Fiction, Non-Fiction, and Expository Text. This strategy can be easily modified for a variety of content areas.

### Grade Level Adaptability

Elementary, Secondary, and Post-Secondary.

### Steps in the Process

1. Ask students to skim and preview the selected text, paying particular attention to text features and structures.
2. Tell students to select important vocabulary terms from the reading, including the brainstorming of possible definitions, synonyms, or antonyms.
3. Divide students into groups of two for the purpose of sharing or modifying terms and definitions.

4. Ask students to use a dictionary, glossary, or thesaurus to verify or modify definitions for selected words.
5. Encourage students to make a non-linguistic representation of each vocabulary word or concept.

## Engage with Bloom's Taxonomy

- *Remember:* What are the most important vocabulary words to remember?
- *Understand:* Using your own words, define the selected terms.
- *Apply:* How could you use this study skills strategy in other subjects?
- *Analyze:* How did you determine which words to select?
- *Evaluate:* How did your selected words and definitions compare to a classmate's selection? Which words were most important? How did you differentiate the importance of each word?

## Benefits

- Allows student choice of words and terms
- Teaches how to use text features and structures
- Straightforward, easy to explain and understand
- Can be done as a pre-reading or post-reading activity
- Can be easily implemented by a substitute teacher
- Fosters independence and interdependence
- Facilitates better preparation for reading expository material as an independent reader

## Considerations

- Students must have workable knowledge of text structures and features.
- May not be challenging for advanced students.
- This strategy may be too time consuming for some students.

## Suggestions for Differentiation

- Use leveled reading material.

- Use flexible student groups.
- Allow additional time for some groups to complete the task.

## Technology Adaptation

1. Ask students to utilize a variety of Internet resources to verify definitions.
2. As a culminating activity, ask students to create an electronic visual representation of the vocabulary terms to share with the class.

## Teacher Notes

_____

_____

_____

_____

_____

_____

_____

_____

## STRATEGY: SELF-ASSESSMENT

### Why Use Self-Assessment Strategy?

The purpose of the Self-Assessment Strategy is to help students become metacognitively aware of their learning strengths and weaknesses related to reading comprehension and study habits.

### Types of Texts

Fiction, Non-Fiction, and Expository Text. This strategy can be easily modified for a variety of content areas.

## Grade Level Adaptability

Upper Elementary, Secondary, and Post-Secondary.

## Steps in the Process

1. Explain to students that the purpose of the strategy is to help them analyze their own reading and studying habits.
2. Ask students to make a written table that includes the following:

**Vocabulary**

| | | | |
|---|---|---|---|
| Do I understand the vocabulary words? | Yes | No | NA |
| Could I explain the meaning of the words? | Yes | No | NA |
| Do I understand the relationships between the words? | Yes | No | NA |
| Does the text glossary provide definitions for all words? | Yes | No | NA |
| Are some vocabulary words more important than others? | Yes | No | NA |

**Comprehension**

| | | | |
|---|---|---|---|
| Can I understand the author's message? | Yes | No | NA |
| Can I follow the organization within the text? | Yes | No | NA |
| Can I solve problems after reading the information? | Yes | No | NA |
| Can I make accurate predictions of the text content? | Yes | No | NA |
| Do I understand why reading the material is important? | Yes | No | NA |
| Can I apply the information from the text? | Yes | No | NA |

**Study Habits**

| | | | |
|---|---|---|---|
| After reading, can I summarize the information? | Yes | No | NA |
| If summarization is difficult, can I fix the problem? | Yes | No | NA |
| Do I have an efficient way to take notes? | Yes | No | NA |
| Do I understand the charts, graphs, etc.? | Yes | No | NA |

Can I organize the information into
an outline?                                       Yes  No  NA
Do I know how to use fix up strategies
when confused?                                    Yes  No  NA

## Engage with Bloom's Taxonomy

- *Remember:* What is the purpose of the self-assessment strategy?
- *Understand:* Explain to a classmate why this strategy helps you understand how to study and read effectively.
- *Apply:* Explain to a classmate why this strategy would be helpful to them.
- *Analyze:* What are other questions that would help you study more efficiently?
- *Evaluate:* Review a classmate's table. Make specific suggestions they could implement in order to study more efficiently.

## Benefits

- Encourages self-reflection
- Supports independent learning across the content fields

## Considerations

- Some students will need more practice with this strategy than other students.

## Technology Adaptation

1. Ask students to create an electronic spreadsheet with the questions and answers.
2. Use Edmodo or Twitter to give feedback to classmates related to their study habits.
3. Ask students to use Glogster to create an electronic display of strategies that work best.

Teacher Notes

_____

_____

_____

_____

_____

_____

_____

## STRATEGY: SELF-MONITORING

### Why Use Self-Monitoring Strategy?

The primary purpose of the Self-Monitoring Strategy (Baker, 1991) is to help students monitor their own comprehension and recognize when a fix-up strategy is necessary.

### Types of Texts

Non-Fiction and Expository Text. This strategy can be easily modified for a variety of content areas.

### Grade Level Adaptability

Elementary, Secondary, and Post-Secondary.

### Steps in the Process

1. Ask students to consider the following questions when reading difficult and challenging text.
   • Are there words I don't understand?
   • Does some of the information contradict what I already know?
   • Do some ideas seem more confusing than others?
   • Is any information missing or unclear?

2. Ask students to read the text while asking themselves these questions.
3. Instruct them to highlight, mark, or identify with a note the most confusing parts of the text.
4. If students are confused by the vocabulary, ask them to write the most challenging words and use the glossary to clarify. They should keep a running list of vocabulary words for each chapter. This list should include non-linguistic representations.
5. If some of the information is contradictory, confusing, missing, or unclear, have students review the subheadings, turn them into questions, and record them.
6. Ask students to look for the answers to the subheading questions within the text. If the text is still confusing, tell students to highlight or mark those sections and seek clarification from the instructor.

## Engage with Bloom's Taxonomy

- *Remember:* What questions should you ask yourself while reading challenging text?
- *Understand:* Explain to a classmate the benefits of asking these questions while reading a text.
- *Apply:* Demonstrate to a classmate how to use this strategy.
- *Analyze:* Compare and contrast this reading strategy with ways you have tried to read difficult text in the past.
- *Evaluate:* Think about this studying method. When will it be useful? When might it not be useful?

## Benefits

- Promotes active reading
- Provides a systematic method for reading the text
- Teaches metacognitive awareness
- Works in a variety of curricular areas
- Uses non-linguistic representation
- Develops a word bank of vocabulary words

## Considerations

- Some students may resist if they have already developed their own method for reading difficult text.
- If everything about the text is confusing, this strategy will be overwhelming.

## Suggestions for Differentiation

- Allow some students to work with a partner.
- Use leveled texts.
- Provide a listening center for some students.
- Provide a graphic organizer for sections of the text.

## Technology Adaptation

1. Ask students to record questions electronically and seek clarification through the use of a class blog.
2. Put individual questions on computers in a computer lab. While using their text, have students rotate through the lab offering clarification to individual questions.

## Teacher Notes

_____

_____

_____

_____

_____

_____

_____

_____

## STRATEGY: SKIM AWAY

### Why Use the Skim Away Strategy?

The purpose of the Skim Away Strategy (Lenski, Wham, Johns, and Caskey, 2007) is to teach students how to skim and scan text in a manner that most supports understanding.

### Types of Texts

Non-Fiction and Expository Text. This strategy can be easily modified for a variety of content areas.

### Grade Level Adaptability

Upper Elementary, Secondary, and Post-Secondary.

### Steps in the Process

1. Explain to students this is a reading strategy that will help them determine the main idea of a text selection.
2. Tell students to open their books, read the chapter title, and glance at the headings and subheadings.
3. Tell students they should consider the main idea as they look at maps, charts, and other graphic organizers.
4. Have students read the chapter summary or conclusion.
5. After students have read the selection, instruct them to close their books and write a paragraph for the purpose of recalling as much information as possible.
6. Ask students to share their paragraphs with a classmate.

### Engage with Bloom's Taxonomy

- *Remember:* What does it mean to skim a reading selection?
- *Understand:* When skimming a text, what should the reader do?
- *Apply:* Explain to a classmate how to use the Skim Away Strategy in another content area.

- *Analyze:* Explain why the Skim Away Strategy is an effective method of reading challenging text.
- *Evaluate:* How could you improve the Skim Away Strategy?

## Benefits

- Helps to activate background knowledge
- Supports understanding and interrelatedness of content within a text
- Facilitates understanding of the importance of text features and structures
- Easily applied to all content areas

## Considerations

- This strategy may be too time consuming for some students.
- Steps in the process may seem repetitive.

## Suggestions for Differentiation

- Compact the reading material for more advanced students.
- Provide graphic organizers.
- Allow students to work individually or with small groups.
- Use leveled text for some students.

## Technology Adaptation

1. Ask students to record notes on a classroom blog.
2. Ask students to record notes over the text using only electronic non-linguistic representations.

## Teacher Notes

_____

_____

_____

_____

## STRATEGY: SURVEY, CONNECT, READ, OUTLINE (SCROL)

### Why Use the SCROL Strategy?

The purpose of the SCROL Strategy (Grant, 1993) is to teach students how to skim and scan text in a manner that most supports understanding.

### Types of Texts

Non-Fiction and Expository Text. This strategy can be easily modified for a variety of content areas.

### Grade Level Adaptability

Upper Elementary, Secondary, and Post-Secondary.

### Steps in the Process

1. Explain to students that they should use scanning, skimming, and more precise reading when reading non-fiction text.
2. Explain that scanning includes looking for specific information. Skimming is when they locate important information and read it quickly. Precise reading is when they slow down the reading rate and carefully consider the content.
3. Ask students to skim the chapter and survey the headings, subheadings, and illustrations.
4. Tell students to share what they learned with a partner. At least one of the partners should record the response.

5. Ask students to share with the class, and have a recorder making a visual display of the information.
6. Ask students to make predictions related to chapter content.
7. Ask students to compare the headings and subheadings and make connections by looking for key words that are the same or have similar meaning.
8. Instruct students to read the text for the purpose of locating information that supports the chapter headings and subheadings.
9. After reading is completed, ask students to make an outline using headings and supporting details.
10. Ask students to compare outlines and verify information in the text.

## Engage with Bloom's Taxonomy

- *Remember:* What do the letters in SCROL represent?
- *Understand:* Summarize how to use the SCROL Strategy.
- *Apply:* Explain to a classmate how to use the SCROL Strategy in another content area.
- *Analyze:* Explain why the SCROL Strategy is an effective method of reading challenging text.
- *Evaluate:* How could you improve the SCROL Strategy?

## Benefits

- Helps to activate background knowledge
- Supports understanding and interrelatedness of content within a text
- Facilitates understanding of the importance of text features and structures
- Easily applied to all content areas

## Considerations

- This strategy may be too time consuming for some students.
- Some steps in the process may seem repetitive.

## Suggestions for Differentiation

- Compact reading material for more advanced students.
- Use graphic organizers.
- Use flexible grouping.

## Technology Adaptation

1. Ask students to record notes on a classroom blog.
2. Ask students to critique classmate work by using Twitter, Edmodo, or Collaborize Classroom.

## Teacher Notes

_____

_____

_____

_____

_____

_____

_____

_____

## STRATEGY: TEXT STRUCTURE

## Why Use Text Structure Strategy?

Using the Text Structure Strategy (Tierney and Readance, 2000) helps students understand how to use features within a text to facilitate understanding and recall of information. While narrative texts usually have a consistent structure, a non-fiction text may have more variety in terms of format.

## Types of Texts

Non-Fiction and Expository Text. This strategy can be easily modified for a variety of content areas.

## Grade Level Adaptability

Elementary and Secondary.

## Steps in the Process

1. At the beginning of the lesson, tell students that authors use the structure of a text to facilitate understanding. Explain that if they don't understand the significance of these features or how to use them advantageously, they may have difficulty focusing, monitoring, and understanding written material.
2. Ask students to divide notebook paper into three equal vertical columns. Tell them to write "Text Structure" at the top of the column on the left and to write "Example" at the top of the middle column. Tell them to write "How This Helps" at the top of the column on the right side of the paper.
3. Ask students to complete the organizer by locating the specific support, giving an example of the support, and explaining how the support helps with comprehension. Sample supports include, but are not limited to the following:
   • Chapter title
   • Headings
   • Subheadings
   • Photos
   • Bold print
   • Italics
   • Diagrams
   • Graphic organizers
   • Author questions
   • Key vocabulary
4. After students have had experience with the graphic organizer for text structures, it may only be necessary to have

them discuss the features of an upcoming chapter as a whole class experience.

5. NOTE: It is recommended students receive instruction in how to use the text structure throughout the school year, using each assigned textbook. This instruction can also be modified for reading material presented online.

## Engage with Bloom's Taxonomy

- *Remember:* Create a text structure graphic organizer.
- *Understand:* Explain to a classmate how to use the graphic organizer.
- *Apply:* Fill in the graphic organizer using a chapter from the text.
- *Analyze:* Explain why the Text Structure Strategy helps with reading comprehension.
- *Evaluate:* How could you improve the Text Structure Strategy?

## Benefits

- Helps students understand the significance of a variety of features on a printed page
- Helps ensure all students have the same advantage when reading difficult text
- Facilitates better preparation for reading expository material as an independent reader
- Can be done individually, with small groups, or with the whole class

## Considerations

- Without the appropriate teacher emphasis, some students will underestimate the importance of text structure related to reading comprehension.

## Suggestions for Differentiation

- Use leveled texts.
- Provide a partially completed graphic organizer for some students.

- Have some students work individually while others work in small groups.
- Provide a teacher-made graphic organizer that includes a variety of text features.

## Technology Adaptation

1. Have students use a PowerPoint to display and share a completed Text Structure graphic organizer.
2. Demonstrate how to use the Text Structure Strategy with online articles.
3. Post a completed Text Structure on a class blog.

## Teacher Notes

_____

_____

_____

_____

_____

_____

_____

_____

_____

## STRATEGY: TITLE, HEADINGS, INTRODUCTION, EVERY FIRST SENTENCE, VISUALS AND VOCABULARY, END OF CHAPTER QUESTIONS, AND SUMMARY (THIEVES)

### Why Use the THIEVES Strategy?

The THIEVES Strategy (Manz, 2002) was designed to help students preview a textbook chapter efficiently.

## Types of Texts

Fiction, Non-Fiction, and Expository Text. This strategy can be easily modified for a variety of content areas.

## Grade Level Adaptability

Elementary, Secondary, and Post-Secondary.

## Steps in the Process

1. Tell students to preview the chapter prior to reading it.
2. Explain the THIEVES acronym.
   - Title—Look at the title, and think about what will be included in the chapter. Think about what is already known about the topic.
   - Headings—Look at the headings. What are the heading topics? Think of ways to turn the heading into a question.
   - Introduction—Read the introductory paragraph and think of what is most important. Anticipate what will be included in the chapter.
   - Every First Sentence—Read every first sentence for each paragraph.
   - Visuals and Vocabulary—Look at photographs, maps, and other graphics. What do they illustrate? Look for important vocabulary words, and define them in the context of the chapter content.
   - End of Chapter Questions—Find the questions in the margins at the end of each section and at the end of the chapter. Keep these questions in mind while reading the text.
   - Summary—Read the chapter summary. Recall what was read.
3. Facilitate student learning by modeling how to use this strategy until such time as they are comfortable with the steps in the process.

## Engage with Bloom's Taxonomy

- *Remember*: What does the acronym THIEVES mean?

- *Understand:* Using your owns words, explain the THIEVES Procedure to a classmate.
- *Apply:* Explain how this study method could be used in other content areas.
- *Analyze:* Think of the steps in the process of the THIEVES Strategy. Why does this strategy work? Why might it not work?
- *Evaluate:* Evaluate the usefulness of this type of study method in math, social studies, science, and English.

## Benefits

- Requires moderate advance preparation from the teacher
- Makes acronyms easy to remember
- Easily adapted for independent studying
- Serves as a study guide for students that lack a successful method of study
- Helps students monitor comprehension

## Considerations

- Some students may resist the method because they view it as too time consuming.

## Suggestions for Differentiation

- Share student responses on a class blog.
- Use flexible time amounts for guided practice.
- Allow students to share information among groups and with individuals.
- Allow students to work with partners or within small groups.

## Technology Adaptation

1. Have students share notes electronically with a class blog.
2. Use WordPress or Blogspot to create a class blog with templates of this process.

## Teacher Notes

_____

_____

_____

_____

_____

_____

_____

_____

## STRATEGY: WHAT'S SO IMPORTANT?

### Why Use the What's So Important Strategy?

The What's So Important Strategy was designed to help students distinguish and note the most important information within a text.

### Types of Texts

Fiction, Non-Fiction, and Expository Text. This strategy can be easily modified for a variety of content areas.

### Grade Level Adaptability

Elementary, Secondary, and Post-Secondary.

### Steps in the Process

1. Tell students not all information within a text is important to remember.
2. Explain that the author of the text designates the most important context through the use of text structure and features. Direct students to pay particular attention to words in italics,

bold print, graphics, words in margins, or questions at the beginning or end of a section.

3. Ask students to design a graphic organizer to facilitate and demonstrate understanding of key vocabulary words.
4. When students have selected words or terminology they believe to be important to their overall understanding, ask them to provide evidence that supports their opinions.

## Engage with Bloom's Taxonomy

- *Remember:* List vocabulary words you consider to be important.
- *Understand:* Paraphrase the definition of each vocabulary word.
- *Apply:* Explain why the understanding of a specific word or term is important to the overall subject.
- *Analyze:* How do the specific vocabulary words help you understand the lesson objectives?
- *Evaluate:* Prioritize the words according to importance within the context of the instructional objectives.

## Benefits

- Can be done individually, with a small group, or with the whole class
- Requires little advance preparation from the teacher
- Provides a ready-made study guide of vocabulary words
- Sets a specific purpose for reading
- Can be easily implemented by a substitute teacher
- Reinforces the importance of structure and features within a text

## Considerations

- This strategy may be too time consuming and less productive for advanced students.

## Suggestions for Differentiation

- Allow students to work individually or in small groups.

- Have students keep a vocabulary notebook of new terms. Students would individually decide which terms to include.
- Ask students to provide a non-linguistic representation of selected words.
- Have students teach their selected words to others in the class.
- Ask students to choose five of the most important words and explain to a classmate why the word was chosen.

## Technology Adaptation

1. Ask students to collaborate and make a vocabulary word study guide to post on a classroom blog.
2. Tell students to communicate with a classmate using Twitter to quiz vocabulary words and definitions.

## Teacher Notes

_____

_____

_____

_____

_____

_____

_____

_____

## STRATEGY: YOUR OWN QUESTIONS

## Why Use the Your Own Questions Strategy?

The purpose of the Your Own Questions Strategy (Vacca and Vacca, 2008) is to help students understand how to understand text content by asking questions related to the text. This strategy will encourage students to think creatively and activate background knowledge.

## Types of Texts

Non-Fiction and Expository Text. This strategy can be easily modified for a variety of content areas.

## Grade Level Adaptability

Elementary, Secondary, and Post-Secondary.

## Steps in the Process

1. Have students read the introductory paragraphs from a text selection.
2. Ask students to write five to ten questions they think will be answered in the remainder of the reading selection.
3. Have students share their questions with a small group or with the whole class. Discuss the types of questions asked and their level according to Bloom's Taxonomy.
4. Display student questions.
5. Ask students to read in order to find the answers to the recorded questions.
6. After reading, ask students to explain which questions were answered, and which questions were not answered, including why questions might not have been answered.

## Engage with Bloom's Taxonomy

- *Remember:* Summarize the steps in the process for Ask Your Own Questions.
- *Understand:* How does this strategy activate background knowledge?
- *Apply:* Explain to a classmate how and when you might use this strategy.
- *Analyze:* Explain why the Ask Your Own Questions Strategy is an effective method of reading challenging text.
- *Evaluate:* Using Bloom's Taxonomy, evaluate the level of questions from classmates.

## Benefits

- Helps to activate background knowledge in a novel manner
- Provides practice with a skill that is easily used by students when working independently
- Easily applied to all content areas
- Provides students opportunity to learn from others
- Supports "conversation" between reader and author

## Considerations

- If students have no background knowledge of subject, developing relevant questions will be challenging.

## Suggestions for Differentiation

- Provide compact reading material for more advanced students.
- Require students to use Bloom's Taxonomy to develop questions.
- Use flexible grouping.
- Use leveled reading material.

## Technology Adaptation

1. Ask students to record questions and answers on a classroom blog.

## Teacher Notes

_____

_____

_____

_____

_____

_____

_____

# Appendix
# ADAPTING WITH TECHNOLOGY

In order to encourage teachers to incorporate the use of technology into the classroom in a way that increases both student engagement and learning, I have included at least one technology adaption for most of the strategies. While none of the strategies *require* the use of technology, all can be *enhanced* through the use technological websites and resources.

The only problem with including technological adaptations within this book is that from the time it is written until the time it is published (approximately six months) new technology resources will be readily available to all educators. Consequently, readers should continue to explore and learn new ways to engage through technology—even when using some of the more traditional teaching methods that support literacy. Most strategies can be slightly modified to make them worthy of a classroom in the twenty-first century, and to not do so would be educational malpractice.

A few of the technological resources currently available to teachers include the following. This list is not comprehensive, but it will help to explain some of the suggestions within the book. It is further recommended that readers of this book follow *Classroom 2.0* on the Internet. This innovative resource is used by many educators on a daily basis.

- Animoto: an online service that helps create videos from images and video clips.
- Blosgpot: allows users to create a simple blog.
- Diigo: an online bookmarking service that supports students as they work on a research project.
- Edmodo: a resource that provides a way to share classroom content in a way similar to Twitter.
- Glogster: an online web service that helps create virtual posters through the use of multimedia.
- Google Docs: a word processing resource to facilitate sharing, creating, and editing documents.
- Google Plus: facilitates the use of video chats.
- Plurk: a social network similar to Twitter.
- Schoology: a website designed to manage lessons, engage students, and share content.
- Shape Collage: facilitates in making an electronic collage.
- Posterous: an easy tool for blogging.
- Teacher Tube: a video sharing website designed specifically for classroom use.
- Tumblr: an easy tool for blogging.
- Twitter: an easy to use microblog.
- Webquest: facilitates students as they research content online.
- Wordle: a resource that generates word clouds from text.
- Zapd: a tool for creating a website.

# BIBLIOGRAPHY

Allen, J. (1999). *Words, words, words: Teaching vocabulary in grades 4–12.* York, ME: Stenhouse.

_____. (2007). *Inside words: Tools for teaching academic vocabulary grades 4–12.* York, ME: Stenhouse.

Anderson, L. W., and Krathwohl, D. R. (eds.). (2001). *A taxonomy for learning, teaching and assessing: A revision of Bloom's Taxonomy of educational objectives.* New York: Longman.

Baker, L. (1991). Metacognition, reading, and science education. In C. Santa and D. E. Alvermann (eds.), *Science learning: Processes and applications* (pp. 12–13). Newark, DE: International Reading Association.

Beck, I. L., McKeown, M. G., Hamilton, R. L., and Kucan, L. (1997). *Questioning the author: An approach for enhancing student engagement with text.* Newark, DE: International Reading Association.

Blachowicz, C. L. Z. (1986). Making connections: Alternatives to the vocabulary notebook. *Journal of Reading 29*, 539–543.

Bromley, K., and Modlo, M. (1997). Using cooperative learning to improve reading and writing in language arts. *Reading and Writing Quarterly 13*(1), 21–35.

Brunner, J. (2009). These kids can't read. *Principal Leadership 9*, 19–22.

_____. (2011). *I don't get it! Helping students understand what they read.* Lanham, MD: Rowman & Littlefield Education.

Buehl, D. R. (1997). Loud and clear: Reading aloud. *The Reading Room*, www .weac.org/news_and_publications/columns,reading_room/index.aspx.

_____. (2001). *Classroom strategies for interactive learning* (2nd ed.). Newark, DE: International Reading Association.

Bulgren, J., and Scanlon, D. (1998). Instructional routines and learning strategies that promote understanding of content area concepts. *Journal of Adolescent and Adult Literacy* 41(4), 292–302.

Cunningham, D., and S. L. Shablak. (1975). Selective reading guide-o-rama: The content teacher's best friend. *Journal of Reading* 18: 380–382.

Dana, C., and Rodriguez, M. (1992). TOAST: A system to study vocabulary. *Reading Research and Instruction* 31, 78–84.

Daniels, H. (1994). *Literature circles: Voice and choice in the student-centered classroom.* New York: Stenhouse Publishing.

Davidson, J. (1982). The group mapping activity for instruction in reading and thinking. *Journal of Reading* 26, 52–56.

De Bono, E. (1994). *De Bono's thinking course* (rev. ed.). New York: Barnes and Noble Books.

Denner, P. R., and McGinley, W. J. (1986). The effects of story-impressions as a prereading/writing activity on story comprehension. *Journal of Educational Research* 82, 320–326.

Eanet, M., and Manzo, A. V. (1976). REAP—A strategy for improving reading, writing/study skills. *Journal of Reading* 19, 647–652.

Ellery, V., and J. L. Rosenbloom. (2011). Sustaining strategic readers: Techniques for supporitng content literacy in grades 6–12. International Reading Association.

Fuentes, P. (1998). Reading comprehension in mathematics. *Clearing House* 72(2), 81–88.

Gillet, J., and Kita, M. J. (1979). Words, kids, and categories. *Reading Teacher* 32, 538–546.

Grant, R. (1993). Strategic training for using text headings to improve students' processing of content. *Journal of Reading* 36, 482–488.

Graves, D., and Hansen, J. (1993). The author's chair. *Language Arts* 60, 176–183.

Haggard, M. (1986). The vocabulary self-collection strategy: Using student interest and world knowledge to enhance vocabulary growth. *Journal of Reading* 29, 634–642.

Hayes, D. A. (1989). Helping students GRASP the knack of writing summaries. *Journal of Reading* 33, 96–101.

Jonson, K. F. (2006). *60 strategies for improving reading comprehension in grades K–8.* Thousand Oaks, CA: Corwin Press.

Klemp, R. (1994). Word storm: Connecting vocabulary to the students' database. *Reading Teacher* 48, 282.

Lamme, L. L., and Beckett, C. (1992). Whole language in an elementary school library media center. ERIC Clearinghouse on Information Resources. ERIC Document Reproduction Service No. ED246874.

Langer, J. A. (1981). From theory to practice: A prereading plan. *Journal of Reading* 25, 152–156.

Lenski, S., Wham, M. A., Johns, J. L., and Caskey, M. M. (2007). *Reading and learning strategies: Middle grades through high school* (3rd ed.). Dubuque, IA: Kendall/Hunt.

Lubliner, S. (2004). Help for struggling upper-grade elementary readers. *Reading Teacher* 57, 430–438.

Manz, S. L. (2002). A strategy for previewing textbooks: Teaching readers to become THIEVES. *Reading Teacher* 55, 434–435.

Manzo, A. (1969). The request procedure. *Journal of Reading* 13, 23–26.

_____. (1975). Guided reading procedure. *Journal of Reading* 18, 287–291.

Manzo, A. V., and Manzo, U. C. (1990). *Content area reading.* New York: Macmillan.

Martin, C. E., Martin, M. A., and O'Brien, D. G. (1984). Spawning ideas for writing in the content areas. *Reading World* 11, 11–15.

Marzano, R. (2004). *Building background knowledge for academic achievement: Research on what works in schools.* Alexandria, VA: Association for Supervision and Curriculum Development.

McLaughlin, M., and Allen, M. B. (2002). *Guided comprehension: A teaching model for grades 3–8.* Newark, DE: International Reading Association.

Moore, D. W., and Moore, S. A. (1992). Possible sentences: An update. In E. K. Dishner, T. W. Bean, J. E. Readence, and D. W. Moore (eds.), *Reading in the content areas: Improving classroom instruction* (3rd ed.) (pp. 196–202). Dubuque, IA: Kendall/Hunt.

Nist, S. L., and Simpson, M. L. (1984). PLAE: A model for planning successful independent learning. *Journal of Reading* 28: 218–223.

Oczkus, L. (2004). *Super six comprehension strategies: 35 lessons and more for reading success.* Norwood, MA: Christopher-Gordon.

Ogle, D. (1986). K-W-L: A teaching model that develops active reading of expository text. *Reading Teacher* 39, 564–570.

Palinscar, A. M., and Brown, A. (1986). Interactive teaching to promote independent learning from text. *Reading Teacher* 39(8), 771–777.

Palmatier, R. A. (1971). Comparison of four notetaking procedures. *Journal of Reading* 14, 235–240.

Pauk, W. (1974). *How to study in college*. Boston: Houghton Mifflin.

Petty, W. T., Herod, C. T., and Stoll, E. (1968). *The state of knowledge about the teaching of vocabulary*. Champaign, IL: National Council of Teachers of English.

Rasinski, T., and Padak, N. (1996). *Holistic reading strategies: Teaching children who find reading difficult*. Englewood Cliffs, NJ: Merrill/Prentice Hall.

Readance, J., Bean, T., and Baldwin, R. S. (1998). *Content area literacy: An integrated approach* (6th ed.). Dubuque, IA: Kendall/Hunt.

Rogers, T. (1991). Students as literary critics: The interpretative experiences, beliefs, and processes of ninth grade students. *Journal of Reading Behavior* 23(4), 391–423.

Rosenbaum, C. (2001). A word map for middle schools: A tool for effective vocabulary instruction. *Journal of Adolescent & Adult Literacy* 45, 44–49.

Ruddell, M. (2005). *Teaching content area reading and writing* (4th ed.). Hoboken, NJ: John Wiley and Sons.

Ryder, R. J., and Graves, Michael F. (2003). *Reading and learning in content areas*. New York: John Wiley and Sons.

Schumaker, J. B., Denton, P. H., and Deshler, D. D. (1984). *The paraphrasing strategy*. Lawrence: University of Kansas Press.

Schwartz, R., and Raphael, T. (1985). Concept of definition: A key to improving students' vocabulary. *Reading Teacher* 39, 198–205.

Simpson, M. L. (1986). PORPE: A writing strategy for studying and learning in the content areas. *Journal of Reading* 29, 407–414.

Slavir, R. (1994). *Educational psychology: Theory and practice*. Boston: Allyn and Bacon.

Spiegel, D. L. (1981). Six alternatives to the directed reading activity. *Reading Teacher* 34, 914–922.

Stauffer, R. G. (1976). *Teaching reading as a thinking process*. New York: Harper & Row.

Steele, J., Meredith, K., and Temple, C. (1998). *Further strategies for promoting critical thinking: Guidebook IV*. Prepared for the Reading and Writing for Critical Thinking Project, a joint collaboration with the University of Northern Iowa, International Reading Association, and the Open Society Institute.

Taba, H. (1967). *Teacher's handbook for elementary social studies.* Reading, MA: Addison-Wesley.

Tierney, R., and Readance, J. (2000). *Reading strategies and practices: A compendium* (5th ed.). Boston: Allyn and Bacon.

_____. (2005). *Reading strategies and practices: A compendium* (6th ed.). Boston: Allyn and Bacon.

Underwood, W. (1987). The body biography: A framework for student writing. *English Journal* 76(8), 44–48.

Unrau, N. (2004). *Content area reading and writing: Fostering literacies in middle and high school cultures.* Upper Saddle River, NJ: Merrill/Prentice Hall.

Vacca, R. T., and Vacca, J. L. (1989). *Content area reading* (3rd ed.). New York: HarperCollins.

_____. (2008). *Content area reading: Literacy and learning across the curriculum* (9th ed.). Boston: Allyn and Bacon.

Wark, D. M. (2007). *General Study Skills: Instant Study Skills.* Retrieved June 29, 2010, from University of Minnesota Counseling and Consulting Services web site: www.uccs.umn.edu/counseling/self_service/study_general.htm.

# ABOUT THE AUTHOR

**Judy Tilton Brunner** serves as clinical faculty in the Department of Reading, Foundations, and Technology at Missouri State University. She is a regular presenter at national and state conferences on the topics of reading, differentiated instruction, classroom management, school safety, and the prevention of bullying behaviors.

CPSIA information can be obtained at www.ICGtesting.com
Printed in the USA
BVOW070941240212

283695BV00002B/4/P